T0365303

THE ART OF LIVING.........

THE ART OF MEDICINE

THE WIT & WISDOM OF LIFE & MEDICINE:
A PHYSICIAN'S PERSPECTIVE

Edward C. Rosenow III, MD, MS

www.trafford.com

North America & international
toll-free: 844-688-6899 (USA & Canada)
fax: 812 355 4082

Dedicated
To my grandchildren
Who have taught me so much

Christian and Kate

ART OF LIVING....THE ART OF MEDICINE

Edward C. Rosenow III, MD, MS

Table of Contents

Before I begin speaking I'd like to say a few things!
Dan Quayle
Vice President
1990

For the last 15 to 20 years I have been collecting Pearls of Wisdom and humorous quotes that have a message, primarily to someday share with my grandchildren. But several years ago, after over 40 years in medicine, I realized that we physicians are losing the ability or desire to practice the Art of Medicine, and as a result, we are losing the public's trust, a personal *sacred trust,* that we have been entrusted and empowered with. We physicians have an awesome responsibility—the momentary complete responsibility for someone else's life, their concerns. The patient comes to us with an implicit trust. We are dealing with life and death, the most intimate of all human interactions. And we are letting our patients down.

In my younger days we referred to the practice of the Art of Medicine as *bedside manner.* Dr Bernard Lown, in his book, refers to the absence of it as *The Lost Art of Healing.* At this point I realized that many of the quotes I saved for my grandchildren fit in with the messages I wish to pass along.

I began to put my thoughts together on what I might tell young physicians about their obligation to the patient, the very reason we are in medicine. *Every day we physicians are given a gift by being invited into a patient's life to make a difference in their life, because they think we care.* When they come to us we are their hosts. By doing this I would urge all physicians to protect the profession and remind them that the covenant of the patient-physician relationship should be their highest priority—they can't do this without practicing the Art of Medicine, every day with every patient.

But it isn't just the patient-physician relationship, *it is the summation of all of our person-to-person relationships that decide whether we are living a fulfilling life.* The Art of Medicine isn't just the perfection of interpersonal trust between the patient and the physician, it involves a caring relationship with the people we work with, our families and our friends, and especially with ourselves. This is *respect, mutual respect!*

I take the golden rule of life one step further in the trust/bonding relationship between the patient and the physician in practicing medicine including the art as well as the science of medicine, and that is:

The Platinum Rule of Medicine:

**Treat every patient like you'd want a
Member of your family treated!**

5

You'll encounter this quote again a few times, as I think it is one of the most important tenets there is in the practice of the art of medicine. If this were done, we wouldn't have nearly as many problems in the practice of medicine as we do. We would restore our lost trust. Our patients deserve to be treated like family. *We are all in this together.* We must treat *all* people with respect and dignity, even if we don't agree with them.

We know, as physicians, that a calcified solitary pulmonary nodule on a chest x-ray is not cancer, that a blood sugar a few milligrams above normal doesn't mean we're immanently going to get diabetes, or a slight elevation in your cholesterol doesn't mean a heart attack is imminent. A woman physician who discovers a breast lump in herself in the morning will likely have an answer as to what it is by late afternoon by self-arranging the appropriate appointments right away. Many women wait 2 to 4 weeks to get this answer, understandably with much anxiety during this time. But to the non physician patient, your family, they frequently think the worst, that their physician might not be telling them everything. Or, the minor abnormality isn't fully explained. They may leave the office feeling worse than when they came in! *Thus, treat every patient as you would want your family treated.* I am adamant on the *Mayo Way* which is

The needs of the patient come first!
WJ Mayo

When I came across Anne Quinlan's statement to the effect that your life is your career, not your work, I realized that unless the physician has a balanced life and not truly enjoying life, then he or she can't effectively practice medicine, the science as well as the art of medicine. Thus, my emphasis on happiness, the art of living.

I am also a strong believer in the importance of a sense of humor. This, and not taking ourselves too seriously, makes us less likely to judge people, to moralize. I think this is mandatory as a stress reliever. *Have you noticed that people laughing together are generally not killing each other!* By using quotes with a message, many being humorous, I think that I can get my point across easier and hopefully my message will last longer. A quote of wisdom or humor says something in a few words or sentences much better in what I and many others would take paragraphs or pages to say. They add to the messages I want to make.

 ♦ **Too many people suffer from terminal seriousness!**

 ♦ **The doctor must have at his command a ready wit as dourness is repulsive both to the healthy and the sick!** (Hippocrates)

I've tried to credit the source of my quotes but frequently by the time they are passed down through a few authors, the name of the originator of the quote is deleted. Most have become anonymous by virtue of this lineage.

Even though I speak as a physician, and although a number of my messages are directed to physicians and other health care workers, the points I try to make are pertinent to *everyone*. Much of what I say here makes for good conversation around the family dinner table.

My hope is that by the public (the patient) reading this, they will get a feeling for what I think they should expect from their physicians as to what the practice of the

Art of Medicine should be, and expect this of their physicians. Then, hopefully, we can ultimately begin to restore the mutual trust we need to improve healing and the health of society.

I summarize the points in my book by saying, "How can I be a better, happier, more productive person?" "How can I leave this world a little bit better?" And, *I wish someone had told me all this when I was younger!*

**What you do today,
Doesn't end today!**

**Nothing would be the same if you
Did not exist!**

David Niven

THE ART OF LIVING....

I finally figured out that the only reason to be Alive is to enjoy it!
Rita Mae Brown

The term 24/7 came to be common jargon just before the turn of the millennium. Newspaper articles and media news talk of 'a society who never sleeps'. We are turning up the treadmill rate to ever faster speeds. And we really don't know why. We are suffering because of it. We're burning the candle at both ends and running out of wax.

> ♦ **Life is what happens when we're busy making other plans!** (John Lennon)

FAMILY, FRIENDS, FUN/FELLOWSHIP, FAITH, FORGIVE, & FORGET............WORK!!!

I'll be repeating this philosophy several times throughout this book because it helps prioritize the *Art of Living*.

In so many ways we are still the 'me generation'. Greed for money, power, position, more free time for personal use, for acceptance by others, has caused us to lose sight of what life is all about. We have become obsessed with achievement, at the same time abandoning our values, our integrity, all for personal gain while subjecting the most important things in our lives—*family, friends and fun*—to lesser importance.

Man will forfeit his health to gain wealth. Then, when he loses his health, will pay anything to get it back!

A person's material possessions become his status symbols, replacing his own self esteem. He's trying to buy his virtues! We've come to expect materialism to fulfill our inner needs, and it can't! How can a new car contribute to our spirituality, our need to be appreciated, to be loved?

> ♦ **We are always getting ready to live but never living!** (Ralph Waldo Emerson)

Instead of doing more we need to concentrate on doing less, while doing what we do better. As a result we can enjoy life, be happier, feel better about ourselves, be better at what we do for a living and even accomplish more. This is especially true for physicians. Only you alone can change your ways. Change must be your choice!

But we never have the time—"I'll do it tomorrow, as soon as I...;" "Wait until I graduate;" "Wait until I get this paper done;" "Wait until after I get this big promotion;" "Wait until we move into our new house;" and so on. Our 'in box' will never be empty, not even at the time of our death.

> ♦ **Your work should <u>not</u> be your career, instead your career should be your life!** (Anne Quinlan)

Many of us just exist, looking ahead to tomorrow's work, and the day and the week after that, filling our mind with concerns of the future without enjoying the day, the moment! I call this *pretraumatic stress syndrome.*

> ♦ **You cannot be first rate in your work if your work is all you have!** (Anne Quinlan)

> ♦ **You cannot take life for granted; life is not a dress rehearsal. It is a classroom, the exam comes at the end!**

As the kids say, *Get a life! A reverence for life!* But you can't get a life alone—you need to love and to be loved. Life is a gift. Savor life! You need to control your life, not your life including your work, controlling you. *Our ability to choose, to direct our lives, is one of our most precious gifts.* Think of life as a terminal illness and you will live it with a joy and a passion. Today. *There is absolutely no promise for tomorrow.*

> ♦ **He had a great life except he never showed up for it!**

Astronomer Hugh Ross once pointed out that the odds of life such as ours forming on a planet are about the same as a tornado going through a large junk yard and leaving a fully functioning 747 ready to fly! This may be an understatement! This subject has been an interest of mine for many years. Just to point out how extremely thin that margin is, the following are some facts that I've come across explaining what is or has been necessary for life:

The *Moon*: without the moon our days would be about 8 hours long, the winds hundreds of miles per hour resulting in only shortened vegetation, no flying animals, and hills—no mountains. Small tides. The Mars size planetesmoid that hit Earth and causing the formation of the earth and the moon shortly after the earth's formation 4.57 billion Years ago, hit only a glancing blow rather than a direct blow, leaving a 1000 mile diameter core of iron in the earth. This iron core produces electromagnetic protection from the solar wind which would otherwise kill us (or prevented life from forming).

Ice rises on formation instead of sinking; otherwise the lakes and oceans would fill up with ice from the bottom up even in warm temperatures.

The *strong force* is the force that holds the nuclei of atoms together and is the strongest force on earth. It is 0.007. If it were 0.006, the force would be too weak and the atom would fly apart. If it were 0.008, the force would be too strong and nuclear fusion couldn't occur—the atom wouldn't split. We wouldn't have suns.

A *supernova* were to occur within 3000 light years from us, the gamma radiation would wipe out all life.

Jupiter: Jupiter's massive size (11 times the size of earth) and strong gravity swept the inner solar system billions of years ago and cleared out billions of asteroids like the rare one it missed that wiped out the dinosaurs 65 millions years ago and more recently Comet Shoemaker Levy 9 in 1994 that it did get. Otherwise Earth would be bombarded constantly.

Our Sun occupies an area in the habitable portion of the Milky Way which is about 2/3rds out from the center. Closer in would expose us to fatal radiation and farther out the suns have too little mass to allow life to develop.

Two-thirds of the estimated sextillion stars in the Universe (estimated to be more stars than grains of sand on Earth) are *binary stars*, meaning 2 (and sometimes 3 stars) are constantly circling each other. This would shove any planet(s) around too close and too far from their sun to establish constancy.

The *Sun's* superb constancy: if its energy production varied by more than 0.25%, we would be too hot or too cold, well beyond tolerance. We live the best distance possible from the Sun, otherwise Earth would be too hot or too cold. Most suns are not this constant.

These are just a few examples that fascinate me. There are many more. Next time you look in the mirror, say to yourself, "I am really lucky to be here. I had better enjoy it!" And just think, if there weren't life like we know it, there wouldn't be hula hoops, the thigh-master, or sit-coms on TV!!!

What counts most in life is what we do for others. This is the essence of living, why we are here. *That you lived, matters*; you've made a difference. Most of what you do for yourself won't be remembered past your death. What good you do for others will be remembered for years and years. This is especially true as it relates to your children and grandchildren. How do you want to be remembered?

The most important things in life aren't things, they're people. We all must have a goal of leaving this world a little bit better than we found it. This is having a purpose in life. Some people go days, weeks, even months without positively affecting the life of others. They don't smile or compliment anyone, or hold the door open for someone; or any other small act of kindness. In fact, they may make life miserable for others. They're critical and negative. At the end of the day, how would you answer the question, *What have you done for anyone today?*

If you have touched one life today, made someone smile
Brought some joy
Complimented someone
Made someone's life a little easier
Then you have justified your being!

Viktor Frankl, in his book *Man's Search for Meaning* that he wrote from his experiences in a concentration camp during WW II, said that the most basic motivating life force is not a quest for power, prestige or wealth, but a search for meaning. A desire to be a better person contributes to this. The physician can and does make a difference every day, some days much more than others, in the lives of the people he or she cares for by maintaining or improving their health, by giving them peace of mind, a sense of well being and hope. No one has the potential to do what the physician can do—*you, the physicians, are unique!* And you will be happier for doing it.

♦ **Machines can decide but we still need doctors to heal!** (Atul Gawande)

Your caring for your patients (and all of us caring for each other) brings true meaning to our lives, satisfying a great human need—ours and our patients. This is the same meaning Frankl was talking about. Think about this.

♦ **Laugh every day. Celebrate!**

Ritualizing happy occasions recognizes something larger than yourself; it brings the family and friends closer around you.

> **If we don't congratulate and celebrate ourselves, we must**
> **Look elsewhere for validation.**
> **This makes us more dependent on others for**
> **Recognition and approval!**
> **Susan Schenkel**

♦ **Show up. Be high on life, on doing good! Have fun! Play!**

If you have ever eaten in a restaurant in Spain or Italy, you generally arrive late in the evening and are expected to stay and enjoy yourselves for hours. There is no planned second seating.

Johnston and Smith in their book *Life is Not Work, Work is Not Life* point out an interesting psychology for playing: "Psychologists note that perfectionists don't play with abandon. Loners are eliminated from most games; suspicious people don't have fun. Depressed (and I would add sleep deprived) individuals don't experience pleasure when it is appropriate. If you want a barometer of your normality, don't check your work patterns—observe your play."

The original title of one of my published papers on the Art of Medicine was *Recertifying in the Art of Medicine,* as a few years ago I predicted that maybe a non profit public interest group might begin to 'grade' their physicians in the Art of Medicine, even putting the results on the internet for everyone to see.

Currently, in most medical specialties, physicians who took their original certifying examination in the science and ethics of their specialty after 1990 received only a time limited certificate good for 10 years. When they recertify after 7 to 10 years, they may someday need a satisfactory patient/peer satisfaction survey result as to the quality of care delivered. Only the patient (and probably peer physicians who work with the physician that is recertifying, and get feedback from their mutual patients) can truly recertify the physician in the art of medicine. It is now looking like the NBME (National Board of Medical Examiners is planning on instituting this for practicing clinicians within the not too distant future. First year medical students now have to take oral exams on "bedside manner". When practicing physicians need to certify (and re-certify at stated intervals), it will only be a matter of time before the results are on a web site. Currently all hospitals that receive any federal funds are judged on the quality of care delivered with certain diseases and conditions with the results on a web site.

Many states maintain physician profiles on a web site and the National Practitioner Data Bank is a product of the federal government designed to track physician discipline which, for the most part doesn't specifically include the *mispractice* of the art of medicine unless it results in a lawsuit, but the public may someday demand more background on the physician(s) they are going to see or just saw. There are various 'bad doctor' web sites out there that come and go.

**I don't care how much he knows
Until I know how much he cares!**

Currently, the ACGME (Accreditation Council of Graduate Medical Education) requires all internal medicine residents to be accredited in the *core competencies*. These cores consist of 6 values:

1) Patient care*
2) Medical knowledge
3) Practice-based learning and improvement
4) Interpersonal and communication skills*
5) Professionalism*
6) Systems-based practice

* These relate to the art of medicine. They can't be tested for on a written quiz; they have to be attested to by their teachers during their 3 years of training before the residents are eligible to take their board examinations. As I stated above it looks like all practicing physicians will eventually be assessed on a regular basis for their core competencies.

A board certificate of competence is not the equivalent of a license to practice medicine but most employers of physicians are now requiring it including hospital practice admissions committees. If someday, this certificate requires demonstration of competence in the practice of the art of medicine, then the physician not adequately practicing the art of medicine may have trouble making a living in patient care. They will have to become *Born Again Physicians!*

Many physicians would feel that this is a further intrusion in their lives, but I argue that I would prefer that organized medicine do this rather than our government!

Hi!

I'm from the government and I'm here to help you!

Some HMOs are offering bonuses to their physician employees based partially on patient satisfaction. Since I wrote the first addition of this book the AMA has signed a pact with Congress to "...develop more than 100 standard measures of performance, which doctors will report to the *federal government* (my italics) in an effort to improve the quality of care". You can see where this is going!

♦ **Government doesn't solve problems, it subsidizes them!** (Ronald Reagan)

However, support personnel who work with the physician, including nurses, the receptionist, and especially the physician residents, can paint a broader picture because 1) they work for extended periods of time with the physician, frequently in the presence of the patient-physician interaction, and 2) very commonly the patient (or the family) ventilate their feelings about the physician to this group, especially if they are unhappy. The patient can ask any one of these people if they would want this particular physician to be their doctor or their family's doctor; the answer is, at least to themselves, almost always a clear yes or no, not maybe. And they might not always know why not; it's a gut feeling from working with a physician over a period of time. This becomes a collection of memories of what patients have told them over time.

Students can rate college faculty on various web sites involving more than 2500 colleges and universities. The majority of the responses are positive. This does 2 things: 1) allows the students to try to avoid the poorer teachers, and 2) gives the college leaders some guidance in improving teaching at their schools. The precedence is set for using the web to anonymously grade someone they relate to!

**The Art of Living is really a continuous process of
Getting used to things we hadn't expected!**

This is maturity, equanimity. More on this later.

A newspaper surveyed 3700 school kids of all ages about how they see adults. A common theme was, "Adults need to slow down, listen more, be less serious and have more fun."

*First I was dying to finish high school and start college.
And then I was dying to finish college and start working.
And then I was dying to marry and have children.
And then I was dying for my children to grow old enough so I could
Return to work.
And then I was dying to retire.
And now, I am dying—and suddenly realize I forgot to live.*

**The question is not whether we will die,
But how we will live!**
Joan Borysenko

The most important person in your life is

YOU

Self-love, my liege, is not so vile a sin as self-neglect!
Shakespeare

♦ **By middle age we are accomplished fugitives from ourselves!** (John Gardner)

Sure, your family, philosophically, is the most important to you, but unless you really like yourself, feel good about yourself, respect yourself, able to forgive yourself, then you can't reach the potential as completely as you'd like to, to love and respect your family, and for that matter, your friends, fellow workers, or your patients. Nor can you expect them to love and respect you. This requires good self esteem. Your success depends on this. You can't enjoy life as much. And you probably aren't as good a physician. *No one is at their best if they don't feel good about themselves.*

♦ **You alone are responsible for your happiness!**

♦ **People will treat and respect you as you treat and respect yourself!**

This is why I think appropriate attire is important in the patient-physician and coworker-physician relationship. For young physicians you only have one chance to make a good first impression. You dress as you respect yourself!

How you dress has nothing to do with your ability to succeed; however, it may affect your success!

Learn to be pleasantly assertive in a non confrontational way. No one can respond to what you don't say. And you will also learn more about yourself.

♦ **What you think of yourself is far more important than what others think of you!**

It is hard to convince teenagers of this but if many (?most) didn't spend a good part of every day trying to impress others, or trying to get into cliques and then keeping others out, trying to be someone they aren't, they would mature and acquire wisdom that much sooner and be happier. *To be themselves, not what they aren't!* The best way for all of us to do this is to practice *kindness*.

I wish my parents would treat and love me
For what I am, rather than for what I didn't become!

♦ **You are what you think, not what you think you are; you alone have complete control over this. This is what makes each of us unique! This is *attitude*!**

Put yourself first—emotionally, physically, intellectually, socially, and spiritually, but unselfishly—to better cope. This is self-preservation. Not to become self-centered, egotistical or narcissistic. *The better you feel about yourself, the better you will feel about other people.* Too many people are handicapped by a dislike of themselves. Strive to reach your potential; the very act of doing this will make you feel good about who you are and where you are going. Concentrate on your strengths rather than struggle with your weaknesses. We *all* have weaknesses! Avoid getting too tired to feel good about yourself.

♦ **Many fears are born of fatigue and loneliness!** (The Desiderata)

At this point, I remind the young people including young physicians that you will make mistakes—it is 100%. Life is a lesson in humility—we are better for it. What is important is 1) how you react to the mistake and deal with it, 2) what you learn from it, and 3) <u>then you forget it!</u> This is resilience and is necessary for survival. These three are all equally important, but it has been said that those truly able to practice the Art of Living are able to not dwell on what has happened in the past. This contributes to your self-esteem. Never allow the negatives to become a part of your thinking. Again, this is attitude. *Move on! Stop watering last year's crop!* And never forget, *This Too Shall Pass!*

**I ain't much but
I'm all I've got!**
Jess Lair

If you are the most important person in your life then

YOUR HEALTH

is your most important asset. Never, never take it for granted. Much of your happiness depends on it. Many people, physicians included, take better care of their cars than they do of themselves—they follow the manufacturer's recommendations!

Get regular health exams. For you young people, and not just physicians, do it every 3 years, and more often the older you get or if there are risk factors. For physicians, do not ask your best friend or your tennis partner to do it. Turn your health care over to someone you trust and don't you direct the testing; and don't self medicate. One reason to have a regular exam by a physician who knows your record is that 15% to 25% of you will have a significant depression in your lifetime. It is not because of anything you did or didn't do, it just happens. Don't put off getting help—do it right away. And again, don't self medicate! If you are depressed you can't effectively practice the Art of Living and certainly not the Art of Medicine. After treatment, you will be a better physician for having been through this.

If it is not already part of the curriculum, I think all 1st year medical students should have a complete physical examination including a flexible sigmoidoscopy, and sit in the waiting room with the other patients. They should also learn how to start their own personal medical file, complete an Advanced Directive as well as an organ donor card.

There are 3 ways of handling stress that I'll deal with in the section on Stress and Burnout, which are especially real problems for physicians, and they are 1) prevent it, 2) deal with it, and 3) ignore it and maybe it'll go away! Of course, preventing it is the most effective and preferred way and this is why coping skills need to be honed in medical school or now if you are beyond medical school to avoid burnout.

Nurturing good friendships is invaluable as a stress reliever and antidepressant. Women do this better than the men. *You can't have friends without being one.* Your health will depend on your level of stress!

> *The best kind of friend is the kind you can sit on a porch and swing with, never say a word, take some deep breaths and then walk away feeling like it was the best conversation you've ever had. Add touching to this, a smile and you will feel rejuvenated and less stressed.*

Exercise daily; we all know its benefits and it can be a great stress reliever, antidepressant and possibly a way of staving off Alzheimer's disease.

> ♦ **I've made enough money, so now I can afford to hire someone to exercise for me!**

You may well be asked to care for physician friends and their families. Doing it half way won't work and you won't be providing adequate care. It is flattering to be asked to do this but think twice before accepting this responsibility, and clarify the expectations ahead of time. Point out that you are to be in charge.

- **The health conscious Californian—arranged to have a sunroof put in his coffin!**

Every physician who has been a patient with a serious illness will tell you he or she is a better physician as a result. Hamilton Jordan, who was President Carter's Chief of Staff, has written on his personal experiences with 3 different cancers in *No Such Thing As A Bad Day.* What he learned and recommends is pertinent to everyone, including physicians (who generally make poor patients). He urges everyone to learn to listen to their body and to act accordingly. Be aggressive, be involved in the decision making, and don't hesitate to get a second opinion, he says. I would add that a caring, competent physician is not offended by this. Don't keep your problems about a serious illness to yourself; instead, get involved in a support group; minimize stress. Write about it. Above all, have a will to live. This requires a positive attitude, a purpose in life.

**If you don't take care of your body,
Where will you live?**
Alice Potter

Usually a discussion of aging (growing older) in most books is put at the end of the book but we know that in many ways we begin to age at around 3 years. Autopsies on late adolescents who died an accidental death disclose in some a significant atherosclerosis of the coronary arteries. For these reasons I don't think it is ever too early or too late to educate ourselves and our children how to minimize many, many conditions that are greatly preventable but not easily treated years later when they occur.

**We could certainly slow down the aging process if it
Had to work its way through Congress first!**
Will Rogers

The following are factors that have been statistically and in some cases, scientifically, confirmed to prolong life, including an association with a positive quality of life:

Happiness	Equanimity
Attitude	Positive relationships
Good health	Sense of humor/laugh every day
Socially active	Spirituality
Optimism	Gratitude
Volunteering	A purpose in life
Exercise	Limited expectations of others

- **The wages of sin are death, but by the time taxes are taken out, it's just a sort of tired feeling!** (Paula Poundstone)

Since this book is about the art of living it is appropriate to discuss what I call the *concepts of growing older,* or what we might refer to as The Art of Growing Older. It is really about *Aging Gracefully.* It is more than what we already know: No smoking, maintain ideal weight, exercise 30 or more minutes 5 days a week, control your lipids, blood sugar and blood pressure and stress. I've learned so much from many patients and older friends and I am grateful to them for their wisdom because they have allowed me to 'look ahead'. In many ways aging is not so much a chronologic factor as it is a biologic one.

> It is naïve, if not unrealistic, to define health as the absence of disease. Better is the concept of wellness, defined as the maintenance of a dynamic equilibrium between one's self and one's environment. You should always emphasize what remains is more important than what is lost.

> Man is endowed with the necessary capabilities to overcome the obstacles set before us every day by our culture. If we are not among the 5% to 10% of the older population with serious disabilities requiring hospital or nursing home care, the responsibility to surmount these obstacles is ours and ours alone. It is our responsibility, not our family's, if we want to remain independant.

♦ **If I knew I was going to live this long, I would have taken better care of myself!**

> Aging is a continuous process of straining the boundaries established by physical, psychological, and social limitations wherever and whenever we meet them. But without pushing them, we will allow ourselves to slip backward into a more dependent state. Social interaction including working, playing, and dialogue with people much younger than us can be a very effective way of staying in step with the times. In this interaction you should not expect them to perform at our perceived biological age level, but instead you should try to interact with them at their level of social and work activity. Do not seek to stay only with individuals in your own age group all the time. *This can be one of the most important concepts of staying young—thinking young!* Never talk to anyone about your medical problems except your doctor. Most people aren't really interested in your health concerns, especially the second time around!

> Therefore, it is important to socialize frequently. Nurture friendships. Make new friends *and accept them for who they are*. The anticipation of a night out with friends and family is a significant source of happiness. But as we will find out, your happiness is up to you, not up to your friends or family. *Contribute to others' happiness; celebrate their successes!*

> *Listen more than you talk.* Ask your friends/acquaintances about themselves. Show a genuine interest in others. This is one of the best ways to make new friends! And never complain!

> Immobility is one of the greatest problems faced by those growing older but it doesn't have to be. They assume that because they are older they should be less physically active and "don't want to bring on a heart attack". On the contrary, it has now been shown in 95 year olds that lifting weights can have a positive

beneficial effect on what an individual can do. Some form of rather strenuous activity, assuming no physical limitations as determined by your physician, should be carried out at least 5 times a week for 30 minutes. It doesn't have to be a continuous 30 minutes.

♦ **May grandmother started walking 5 miles a day when she was 65. She's now 70 and we don't know where the heck she is!** (Ellen Degeneres)

Immobility begets more immobility to the point that the individual becomes more sedentary, gains weight, in turn is less socially active, and so on. I think that voluntary inactivity is a major contributor to immobility, resulting in a self-limiting life in a wheel chair or on a walker. This results in weight gain, falls, fractures, insecurity, and further immobility, promoting more inactivity.

You know you're getting older when you bend down to get
Something off the floor and you ask yourself, "Is there anything
Else I can do while I'm down here!"

<u>Any</u> reasonable physical exercise with which you can maintain and improve your leg muscle strength, such as stair climbing, would be extremely beneficial. If you live in a high-rise, climb one to three flights of stairs one to three times a day and take the elevator down. Going downstairs is hard on the knees and other dependent joints and doesn't gain you much. Or, sit in a straight chair and get up and out of it five to ten times one to five times a day without using your arms to push off—it works! Join an exercise class. Walk!!! Use a cane if you are uncertain of your balance.

➤ No matter how active we are, we lose 1% muscle mass per year. And with immobility for any reason, this can be up to 2% to 3% per year beginning at age 25. With a chronic wasting illness the loss of muscle mass will be even greater.

➤ It is becoming evident that even people of ideal weight through their pre-senior years tend to gain weight later in life. Watch this! Even if you are the same weight at 70 as you were at 50, this means that you have put on extra fat to replace the muscle you have lost. If you are overweight, it is never too late to lose weight, sensibly. You can't do this without exercising. Eating right is imperative.

➤ The asset of wisdom is an exclusive for the older person, as 'there is no such thing as a wise young man'. Bringing your experience to bear on psychological, social and political issues in our culture is an obligation as well as a privilege. VOTE! Mentoring others is one of the most valuable things you can do; it is the passing along of a lifetime of wisdom through your experiences. It will be a legacy of you.

Death and taxes are inevitable, but death doesn't get worse
Every time Congress meets!
Will Rogers

➢ Extra rest during the day is the oldest form of therapy there is. It is not necessary to have a physical problem to use rest therapy. In fact, quiet resting (precious solitude), lying down for 30 to 40 minutes every early afternoon, can rejuvenate you. It is not necessary to sleep; instead, read, listen to music, or just enjoy the quiet while thinking good thoughts. More and more senior people are into yoga and meditation. There are no negatives to these!

➢ Growing older gives us the opportunity to pursue new goals and achievements made available to us only because of growing older. Go back to school to learn new skills including computer skills. Emailing your grandchildren and even great grandchildren will keep you young! Develop new hobbies but don't wait until you retire. Your experience at this stage of life can be invaluable as a volunteer to one or more organizations. There is no better way of building self-esteem than volunteering. There are very few volunteer organizations that require heavy physical work. What you can contribute could be beyond what they could purchase if they had the money. And take a grandchild or two with you; what you teach them can't be learned any other way. Remember what I said about mentoring. Get involved in school programs helping children read, tutoring them in skills that maybe you have but the schools don't!

How many years we have left is of much less significance
Than what we are going to do today. The
Quality of our days is more important than the quantity!

➢ Remaining mentally active is extremely important, almost imperative. Passively viewing television all day will have a detrimental effect. Just as an athlete must keep his or her muscles in good physical condition, so must you keep your mind sharp with active use of it. Read every day. Pursue hobbies. *Challenge yourself!*

➢ Teach yourself to think (if you haven't already done so!). When you put your keys or anything else down, close your eyes for 1 second and think what you are doing. Make notes to yourself; in this complicated world we have to do that. Keep a calendar of upcoming events. Write down names of people whose names you tend to forget and go over the list every so often. *Vary your routine*. Be more flexible in your day to day activities, rather than rigid and set in your ways.

➢ As you get older frequently ask yourself if you are a safe driver. Are your grandchildren safe with you? Don't be stubborn—listen to the advice of your children/grandchildren and friends. Don't make life hard for them! In fact, ask yourself, "What can I do to make life easier for them?", and I don't mean giving them money. If they say it is not safe for you to continue to drive or do something else, abide by their wishes. Make a list of what you want each child or grandchild to get of your possessions and discuss this ahead of time. Not doing this can be very divisive within your family after you are gone and will leave negative memories of you. *How do you want to be remembered?*

There is the story of the 92 year old, petite, well-poised and proud man, who is fully dressed each morning by eight o'clock, with his hair fashionably coifed and perfectly shaved, even though he is legally blind, moved to a nursing home today. His wife of 70 years recently passed away, making the move necessary. After many hours of waiting patiently in the lobby of the nursing home, he smiled sweetly when told his room was ready.

As he maneuvered his walker to the elevator, he was provided a visual description of his tiny room, including the curtains hung by his window. "I love it," he stated with the enthusiasm of an eight-year old having just been presented with a new puppy.

"Mr. Jones, you haven't seen the room; just wait."

"That doesn't have anything to do with it," he replied. "Happiness is something you decide on ahead of time. Whether I like my room or not doesn't depend on how the furniture is arranged...it's how I arrange my mind. I already decided to love it. It's a decision I make every morning which I wake up. I have a choice: I can spend the day in bed recounting the difficulty I have with parts of my body that no longer work, or get out of bed and be thankful for the ones that do."

"Each day is a gift, as long as my eyes open I'll focus on the new day and all the happy memories I've stored away. Just for this time in my life."

"Old age is like a bank account. You withdraw from what you've put in. So, my advice to you would be to deposit a lot of happiness in the bank account of memories. Thank you for your part in filling my Memory Bank. I am still depositing."

♦ **Wisdom may be the single best predictor of aging well!**

Finally, never be negative. NO ONE likes to be around complaining, grumpy, negative people. You'll lose all your friends. Ask yourself, "Am I a complainer?" If you think you are, write out in big print on a card and put it on your bathroom mirror saying, *"Never complain."*

REMEMBER: ENJOY LIFE, YOU'VE EARNED IT!

HAPPINESS

**"As Miss America, my goal is to bring peace to the
entire world and then get my own apartment!"
Jay Leno**

You must get your priorities straight! If you want happiness, your family and friends and you come first. This is putting *balance* in your life—one of the most important things you can do. I can't stress this enough. Balance isn't 'either/or', it's *'and'*. You know you are leading a balanced life when you function as well when things are going bad as when they are going good and your overall perspective and satisfaction with life remains nearly the same. Life, as you experience it, is a compilation of a series of averages; it is estimated that we have 20,000 experiences every day! Ideally, the very vast majority of these experiences are registered as a positive event, an event "containing" happiness. It is your memories and the end-point of these events that brings happiness. When you return from a trip, would you go again? (happy experience), or are you really glad you are home? (unhappy experience). Maybe your are glad you went but not likely to take that trip again; but still have very happy memories of the trip. It is this summary that you will remember.

We have learned so much about happiness and other human experiences in the last few decades than we have in the last 200 years. And that is because we can finally measure something, namely endorphins, cortisol, blood coagulants, and immunoglobulins in the blood and see something on a brain PET scan or functional MRI of the brain. To me as a scientist as well as a firm believer of the art of living, which spreads over to the art of medicine, these new findings are awesome and just the beginning. Maybe someday we can use these chemicals that I call *happy hormones to* induce happiness in people. This would be unfortunate, though, as you need to achieve happiness through your own thinking and actions. But happy hormones may get you started and then you continue without them and maintain happiness through your own intentions. What I am saying, though, is that a good mood is a biochemical phenomenon.

I'm going to cover this new *Science of Caring* later in my book as well as in my section on *The Qualities of the Respected Physician,* and *The Mayo Culture of Caring* where I feel that Mayo's 100 plus years of success is largely due to factors of decades of a caring culture that, if we wanted to, could be quantified in the blood or MRI of the thousands of employees, not just the doctors, if we so wished. I have put the section on Happiness in the Art of Living section because I think it transcends all of the qualities I've listed under the *Qualities of the Respected Person*, but I'll allude to the quality of happiness throughout my book.

**The more we attain,
The emptier we become!**

Martin Seligman in his book *Authentic Happiness* and his web site www.reflectivehappiness.com and other psychologists are making a science of the study of happiness.

Don't buy unnecessary material things, instead buy experiencing things like trips, exercise equipment, health club membership or gifts of money and time to those truly in need.

- ♦ **Always borrow from a pessimist—they don't expect to be paid back anyway!**

To show you how serious the subject of happiness has become there is a journal of Happiness Studies. Some psychiatry departments in academic medical centers have a section on happiness, after the realization that rather than put 100% of their effort on researching and dealing with depression, personality disorders, psychosis, drug addiction, maybe we should find out about the other end of the spectrum!

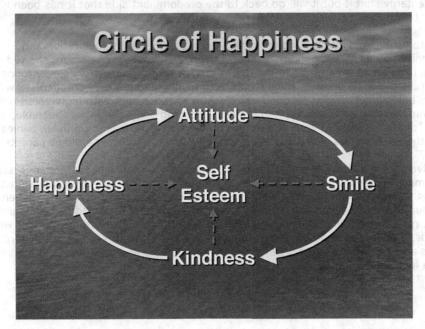

From my extensive reading I have found this Circle of Happiness to be very instructional. This exact circle is mine but the concept isn't original. To get to happiness, you have to begin with Attitude and Kindness, both of which will be covered later. We know now that this circle is hard-wired, truly hardwired in various but connecting areas of the brain.

We each have over 100 billion brain cells and each cell has many hundreds of connections with further extensive networking to multiple areas of the brain. The brain isn't just 'the brain,' instead there are many dozens of areas within the brain, ranging from a few millimeters in size in the brain stem to the cerebral cortex weighing a few pounds. The 'brain' includes the primitive brain that the lower animals live on but in humans still controls all our autonomic (automatic) functions like breathing and sleeping and even some emotions. Our brain is the biggest computer there is. As a result, the hard wiring in our brain is difficult to unwire and re-wire.

The good news is that the individual has control over this and with months (maybe years in some people) of intent to re-wire the circle, it can be done. It might take professional help in certain people to accomplish this but is definitely doable. Drugs alone aren't the answer.

The use of the PET scan and functional MRI have been awesome in defining what is going on in our brains. We now know that the level of happiness resides in the left prefrontal cortex of the brain (just behind the forehead bone) as seen on an MRI, while negativity and 'prepare for an attack' lies within the right prefrontal cortex (and the amygdala in the primitive brain). It can't be on both sides at same time. You can momentarily shift it but it will go back to the predominant side that it has been hard-wired to until you re-wire it.

An interesting study on a Buddha monk, who was a master of meditation and recognized by all that knew him as a very happy, calm, resilient person, showed on MRI a highlighted area as far to the left in the left prefrontal cortex as ever found in hundreds of people studied. Babies born with highlighted left prefrontal cortex were happy babies, not colicky, "a good baby" whereas those born with highlighted right prefrontal cortex were colicky, had difficulty sleeping and eating, were irritable, and were "difficult babies". These are studies on newborns. Following up these babies over the years will be of great interest as well as studies of their biologic parents.

Positive personal social contact is also one of the most important features necessary in human mental and physical well-being. This is fellowship. You can't truly network unless you are social and some will tell you that certain aspects of success depends on your ability to network. It requires a mutual sacrifice of time and self pleasures (e.g., reading, hobbies). You can be efficient with time and with things but not with friends. It is an exchange of caring. It says, "We are not in this alone; let's share our hopes and aspirations, our joys and sorrow, our defeats and frustrations." For some it is a form of spirituality.

- ◆ **The better we get along with people the better we feel about ourselves!**

Making people feel important and happy makes you feel better. You can't contribute to others' happiness if you aren't happy. This is most important in your family's happiness. How can you expect your children to be happy if you aren't!!! When someone asks you what you would like your children to be in their adult life, meaning what kind of occupation, after thinking about it for a few moments, you would eventually say, that it is unimportant what they do as long as they are happy!

Don't Worry, Be Happy!

(song by Bobby McFerrin)

HAVE FUN!

No one guarantees you **happiness**, only you can, but the Bill of Rights does guarantee you the right to pursue happiness. Some would say you aren't truly a success unless you are happy and at peace with yourself. To turn this around, if you equate happiness with your and societies' definition of success, you may never achieve the amount of success necessary to make you happy.

Happiness is the meaning and purpose of life!
Aristotle

**The very purpose of our life is to seek
Happiness, something better in life!
Dalai Lama**

These quotes may sound selfish and self centered but, on the contrary, the happy person makes the people around him or her happier and more productive. In fact, you have an *obligation* to be happy! A happy physician has more cooperation from his or her patients and better outcomes. The happy person is also much more inclined to do good and be kinder than those who are unhappy, who are, indeed, more likely to be self centered and narcissistic and lonely. Happiness is an attitude, as noted in the Circle of Happiness, an inner discipline, and can occur only within the person. To actively seek it causes you to lose it. And it can't be given to you. Instead, just recognize your own contentment and serenity, your peace of mind. Greed destroys happiness, as the greedy person seeks something outside himself in search of happiness. Greed becomes tremendously addicting.

♦ **Cooperation is doing with a smile what you have to do anyway!**

Nadine Crenshaw in her book *The Art of Living. Simple Wisdom for the Self* points out that the present moment is priceless. She says that people that enjoy life tend to live quiet lives, loving each other and the world around them, that they have been able to let go of guilt, fear and negativity. They also accept that life isn't always fair and so they never feel like a victim.

In another book by Foster and Hicks *How We Choose to Be Happy* they further add to Crenshaw's definition by saying that happiness is *a profound enduring feeling of contentment, a centeredness…a rich sense of well-being that comes from knowing you can deal productively with all that life offers you—both the good and the bad.* As we'll see, these definitions closely jibe with good self-esteem, as in the center of the Circle of Happiness.

Happy people are flexible, unassuming, able to feel deeply; they have a passion and move through life with a grace, an elegance, a warmth. *And most have a sense of purpose in life.* They practice mindfulness.

For Foster and Hicks to research the material for their book, they interviewed hundreds of people whose peers said they were the happiest people they knew. As a result, they came up with *The 9 Choices of Extremely Happy People,* and are as follows:

1) <u>Intention</u>, a desire and commitment to be happy, which is a daily purposeful action. *It's the only day you've got—why have a bad one!* Is an attitude.
2) <u>Accountability</u>. We alone are responsible for our actions, our happiness.
3) <u>Identification</u> is the process of assessing yourself as to what makes you happy.
4) <u>Centralizing</u>, honoring your internal values, needs and interests which may require taking risks.
5) <u>Recasting</u>, taking control of your emotions. A resilience. 'Emotionally capable'. (I would add that this might take professional help.) Recasting helps to restore happiness when it has been temporarily taken away.

6) <u>Options</u>. Open minded. Flexible. Don't assume anything; don't make automatic decisions. Requires mindfulness.
7) <u>Appreciation</u>. There is always something to appreciate. By being appreciative you become more empathetic.
8) <u>Giving</u>. (I would add giving of yourself--volunteering.)
9) <u>Truthfulness</u>

Happy people average 2 to 5 days a month of 'not being happy' but not necessarily being unhappy. We are generally less happy at around 8 in the morning—we just have to live with this. At 8 AM our blood cortisol levels are at their lowest in the 24 hour period and may be a contributing factor. (see section on Science of caring)
I don't know when the low level of happiness is in people who work the swing and night shifts, which is a huge population in our country.

♦ Life is a banquet—are you starving?

However, it has been said that one of the comforts of happiness is that you don't have to be happy all the time. No one can. But knowing this should help. Realize when you are low and avoid making major decisions then.

The greater the level of calmness and peace of mind, and the lack of a tendency to compare yourself unfavorably to others, the greater the likelihood of achieving happiness. Comparison is one of the roots of unhappiness. Power is not happiness. People in power usually want more power, power over people and money. Power becomes an obsession. You frequently have to give up something to get and keep power, including friendships, and eventually your integrity.

I've extracted some of these ideas from numerous books and articles I've read on the subject of happiness and joy and most say pretty much the same thing. It is the ability to take pleasure in life's little treasures, today, to give yourself to others, to maintain only positive thoughts, and maybe most importantly to have several close *friends.* All these are essential to achieving happiness. This isn't always easy and requires a dedication to these principles, but it is doable and must be worked at. Unhappiness comes easier than happiness if you are fixated on negative thoughts!

♦ Happiness is a journey, not a destination! It is not a goal, it is a by-product!

Happiness is not the absence of problems, it is how you handle them! Don't confuse happiness with comfort or luxury. A lot of your happiness depends on your philosophy of life; I suggest you write this out (more on Write-Therapy later). And, of course, a lot of it depends on your health.

Happiness is the best face lift!

Dennis Prager in his book *Happiness Is A Serious Problem* states that our philosophy of life should be a thought out ahead of time response to the adverse events of life that <u>everyone</u> will experience such as bad luck, missed opportunities, accidents, illnesses, deaths, financial setbacks, thefts, etc. I see this as a maturation process. But you must be prepared to deal with them when they occur. And if you have written this out, you will know what to do.

- **No one promised you a rose garden............because there is *NO* rose garden!**

Real joy comes not from ease or riches or from the Praise of men, but from doing something worthwhile!
Sir Wilfred Grenfell

To be without some of the things you want is an Indispensable part of happiness!
Sir Bertrand Russell

Happiness is not a chronic state of euphoria, the momentary feeling you have when you get a real good grade in school, or your first love, or get the job or promotion you have worked hard for. It is more a sense of well being, a state of heightened consciousness, a true awareness of appreciation, a peace of mind. Some would describe it as a deep spiritual experience. It is always seeing some, maybe a lot, of good in everyone. This is what 'the glass is half full means'. Live it. Learning to live in the present moment (mindfulness) is absolutely necessary for happiness. Dan Baker in his book *What Happy People Know* describes it as the feeling that comes from deeper sources from awareness of and acting on your virtues and strengths, the kindnesses we show others and ourselves. Some describe it as a spiritual experience. *We are what we think!*

If you want others to be happy, practice Compassion. If you want to be happy, Practice compassion!
Dalai Lama

Some researchers estimate that 50% of anyone's happiness is determined through their genes and that through a combination of genes, upbringing and social pressures we are thought to have a set point of level of happiness and can't do anything about it. Cutler's book on *The Art of Happiness* where he interviewed the Dalai Lama is more encouraging and I agree as now do a number of psychologists specializing in happiness. I know we can do something about our own level of happiness. In fact many people become less happy (below their set point) through constant negative thinking, concentrating only on themselves, blaming others for their problems.

It is imperative that we appreciate that negative thoughts and emotions are counter productive and harmful to achieving happiness and joy, per the Circle of Happiness, but this can take months and years to overcome. *But it can be done*. It must be done! Share your happiness; put it in your voice, your actions, your smile. Be cheerful. You owe it to your family!

Most folks are about as happy as they make up their minds to be!
Abraham Lincoln

Savor the *little* victories, the little acts of kindness you've done or witnessed, watching a sunset, the joy of a family gathering, your child's first steps and words, the patients you have helped. Visually photograph these into your memory bank. These should add up to much more than a raise, a promotion, the success of a paper

27

published. *Don't postpone joy!* Celebrate today! Celebrate the little accomplishments. Don't forget, *the most important things in life aren't things!* **They're people!**

We know that the memory of some of these little things last only about 2 weeks, so write them down and occasionally look at them. Count your blessings, on paper. Or put them on the back of a photograph of your family, or pet or nature scene and carry this with you. Look at it several times a day.

In fact, there is a form of self-therapy towards happiness that is proving very effective and that is *gratitude journaling* whereby every week you write down what you are grateful for. You have to write it out—just thinking it won't work nearly as well. Why not do it every evening at bedtime? Just a few things and build on these. One reason to do it this way is that the subconscious works 24 hours a day and while you are sleeping, these positive thoughts are being worked on and ready for you in the morning. You are being re-wired into a positive attitude and ultimately kindness while you sleep!

They will be uplifting and serve to remind you of the many things you have to be thankful for, bringing you an inner joy and contentment, even if momentary. These acts of appreciation for what you have suppresses negative thinking. The more you do it, the more you suppress these energy sapping thoughts.

Another thing you can do is at least 5 acts of kindness a week. And write these down if you wish. How do you know if it is an act of kindness? You'll know.

> **What a wonderful life I've had.**
> **I only wish I realized it sooner!**
> **Colette**

Prager goes on to point out that for you to be happy you need a cheerful disposition, emotional intelligence and to always be striving for excellence, but never for perfection because you won't get it. He lists 7 concepts we need to accept in order to achieve happiness and they are

1) This too shall pass
2) That which doesn't kill me makes me stronger
3) There is a silver lining to most things
4) To live is to suffer
5) God allows unjust suffering
6) We are blessed in spite of suffering—others have it a lot worse
7) Belief in an after-life

Not everyone would agree with all of these but for the most part I think he is correct. The first 6 state what we intuitively know, but putting them all together puts them in to some context, providing you accept them. I would add number 8 as someone to love and to be loved, number 9 as the willingness to change, and number 10, *friends!*

It's becoming evident that having good **friends**, not just acquaintances, but real friends are essential to happiness, with some saying it is the most important. Diener and Seligman found that in surveying people about happiness the top 10% of students with the highest levels of happiness and least signs of depression rated close ties with friends as their reason for being happy!

**Of all the things that wisdom provides to help one's
Entire life in happiness, the greatest by far is friendship!
Epicurus**

Good friends don't just happen. There is probably a chemistry that brings you together, but eventually over time, a love of caring for each other subplants the chemistry. An almost indispensable connection takes place that usually lasts a lifetime.

♦ **You have to be a friend before you can have a friend!**

How many close friends can you have? There is a limit, some say 5 to7. But in fact it is not likely all 5 to 7 will have the same chemistry for each other, requiring you to work at your various friendships and it does take work, a lot of work. Maintaining good friendships doesn't just happen. We have to remember that people change, just as you change as you get older. Are you prepared to accept this? You must persist in the mutual respect you have for each other through good and bad times.

♦ **A friend is a person who knows all about you but likes you anyway!**

If you were another person, would you like to be a friend of yours? It takes an element of maturity to accept the vagaries of the personalities of some of your friends, but this makes life interesting. It is like a marriage—you have to commit and to communicate. *Knowing how to keep a friend is more important than gaining a new one!*

♦ **Everyone seems so normal....until you get to know them!**

Alice Potter in her book *Positive Thinkers' 10 Commandments* lists a number of 'commandments' of friendship:
1) Be there when needed
2) Listen
3) Only give advice when asked
4) Criticize carefully
5) Tolerant, not judgmental
6) Show appreciation
7) Be kind
8) Believe in
9) Keep your promises
10) Don't gossip
11) Forgive
12) Be yourself

♦ **The time to make friends is before you need them!**

I will add some thoughts to Alice Potter's:
❖ With my best friend I can do anything or nothing and have the best time.

- ❖ Know when your friend is in need.
- ❖ The best thing I can give a hurting friend is my presence, not my words.
- ❖ When you're too busy for your friends, you're too busy. And maybe they are not you friends.
- ❖ Friends are like flowers—they brighten your day!
- ❖ Share and celebrate their joys, share their sorrows. Be there for them.
- ❖ Friendship is the voluntary discipline of ignoring faults in one another.
- ❖ You're never a failure if you have friends.
- ❖ It is ideal to have a close friend or two of the opposite sex.
- ❖ Some of the best marriages are when your spouse is your very best friend.

◆ A friend is someone with whom you can be yourself!

Being yourself takes great courage. Friendship entails trust, mutual trust. This is critical. People are enriched, feel good and are happier when friends trust friends. It creates a connection, a bonding that can be unique.

◆ A true friend never gets in your way unless you happen to be going down!

Members of your immediate family can be best friends but again, it is most commonly to be just one or two of them. Maybe it is a chemistry thing. Or, is sibling rivalry a factor with brothers and sisters? It is probably more than that.

Your children should be one of your greatest sources of happiness and in many families this is true. One study showed that children are 4 times more likely to be listed as a great source of happiness compared to the spouse!

◆ Mental illness is inherited—I got it from my children!

CHILDREN!
Tired of being harassed by your stupid parents?
ACT NOW
Move Out! Get a Job!
Pay your own bills while you still know EVERYTHING!

◆ What we want is for things to remain the same but get better!
(Sidney J. Harris)

Usually things don't get better without initiating or accepting some change. Prager further adds that happiness is not so much a primary state of mind as much as it is a by product of several things:

- A passion for life, for meaningful pursuits
- A depth in an endeavor to grow in all ways, seeking maturation and wisdom, willing to forgive and forget
- Understanding yourself and your life
- A sense of goodness that leads to peace of mind and a sense of self-worth

I think the importance of passion is underestimated. It is a demonstrated, but not necessarily vocal, enthusiasm for everything around you; a disciplined commitment to grow and to be involved in other peoples' lives. It is being non complacent with the status quo. Passion takes energy but ultimately the return is greater than the output. It raises joy and happiness to a new level.

The reverse of passion might be procrastination, an almost disciplined passivity to not deal with problems and the necessary decisions to be made <u>now</u>, based on the thinking that if you ignore them they'll go away, which is rarely the case. If they don't put off making a decision, the unhappy person embarks on an exhaustive search for every option before finally making a tenuous decision.

> ♦ **Nothing is more difficult, therefore more precious than to be able to decide!** (Napoleon)

Chronic procrastination can contribute or maybe even cause a depression (sometimes it might be difficult to know which comes first). We can talk ourselves into thinking that we have nothing in our 'in box' that requires a decision now and that maybe we can be free of any dilemmas that need some action for a day or so (false expectations). But don't allow yourself to think this way—something may come up in the next 5 minutes, leading to disappointment that you have to make more decisions, or procrastinate on them. Not handling it now weighs on you and puts you into analytic thinking about it, shifting your energies into worrying about the future rather than enjoying the present.

> ♦ **It is not that they don't know the solution; it's that they don't see the problem!** (CF Chesterfield)

Joy and happiness are not quite the same thing. You can be unhappy about something and still joyful. I see joy as a deeper sense of happiness. It is a feeling of commonality among all living things; a realization of a conscious spirituality, of something more than material things. The feeling you get when you give of yourself to help others. Some would describe joy as the ultimate expression of gratitude and appreciation connecting us to the whole wondrous world, not just your little world. This may be maturity at its greatest. Money can't buy joy and happiness, so spend your time doing things you *enjoy!*

> ♦ **You never see a hearse pulling a U-Haul!**

> ♦ **Whoever said money can't buy happiness isn't spending it right!**

At the funeral a friend asked the deceased's banker, "How much did he leave?" The banker replied, "He left it all!"

> ♦ **We do not see things as they are, we see them as we are!**

People get so busy blaming others they forget to solve the problem.

> ♦ **He who cannot dance puts the blame on the floor!** (Hindu proverb)

This statement says that some people live in a 'depersonalized-by-blame' world. We have become a society of entitlement, one of 'victim-thinking'. It's someone else's fault that we're not happy, or able to hold a job. When we live in the blame-state, we can't learn, can't change, don't mature. *Blame is a call to anger!* These people will never know joy and happiness. They live in a little negative world of their own making. *Maturity is the ability and desire to take responsibility for your actions.*

> ♦ **It's just a bad day; it's not a bad life!** (Patti Hegdal)

Joy and hope are intertwined. The joyful person always has hope (optimism). This lessens stress and depression.

David Snowdon studied nearly 700 nuns (*Aging with Grace: What the Nun Study Teaches Us About Leading Longer, Healthier, and More Meaningful Lives*) and found some very enlightening facts. Before the novitiates embarked on their careers, they wrote out their short life histories, their wishes and their desires. These files were reviewed many years later and Snowdon found that those with a positive attitude and imbued with optimism were living at least 10 years longer than those with negative attitudes. Lifestyles were the same in all and thus didn't confound the outcome. There is a real message here!

> ♦ **From another optimist: "We're surrounded. Now we can attack in any direction we want."**

The following are statements about joy that I've collected from various authors including Hede Marker who wrote *Joy and Inner Peace.* I think the ability to experience joy is a sign of appreciable maturity.

The joyful person
   Is able to
- Think and act spontaneously rather than on fears based on past experiences, and always based on your integrity
- Be **passionate** about people and things
- Experience a stillness and a sense of peace and a warm sense of satisfaction
- Appreciate a sense of pride
- Have feelings of connectedness with people and with nature
- Allow him or herself to be loved (and to love), because they know they deserve it
- Enjoy each moment, **have FUN**

Having fun is not a luxury; you deserve it—believe this! Fun is a relief from stress, and you'll live longer. Ideally, almost everything you do should be fun, enjoyable. What is the definition of fun? It is one of those things you don't need a description of. But you have to relax and let loose of some of your preconceived inhibitions! You have to stop and think, *I am having fun!* Note, this is in the present tense.

The joyful person
   Has
- Overwhelming urges at times to smile
- Increased tendency to let things happen rather than try to make them happen
- Intense episodes of appreciation
- A feeling of contentment and cheerfulness
- Direction, knowing exactly what you want and pursuing it

The joyful person
Has lost interest in
- Judging other people
- Interpreting the actions of others
- Conflict
- The ability to worry
- Comparing him or herself to others
- Expecting too much of other people

- ◆ **If something unpleasant happens, you have 2 choices: if there is something you can do about it, do it and don't worry. If there is nothing you can do about it, don't worry!**

- ◆ **Don't tell me worrying doesn't work. I know better, because the things I worry about never happen!** (Mark Twain)

I don't think you can maximize your happiness without simplifying your life. I'll discuss this in the section on stress. More thoughts, these on happiness.

Happiness

- Seek happiness as the 11th commandment
- The secret of happiness is something to do, people to love, to be loved, something to hope for, being satisfied with yourself

- ◆ **If you can't be happy here and now, you never will be!**

- Only people can make you happy
- Is directly proportional to how you relate to others
- Do something every day you don't want to do—don't procrastinate
- Strive towards meaningful goals, even if you don't achieve all of them
- The way to be happy is to make others so
- Make a list of your blessings and look at them frequently (see section on Write-Therapy)
- Able to think about other things after a disappointing event—this is resilience.
- Don't look back. Don't ask, "What if?" except to learn and then move on
- Can be as habitual as gloominess
- Feelings of gratitude is essential

- ◆ **The more gratitude you have the more blessings you have to be grateful for!**

- ◆ **Why should God give you more if you are not grateful for what you have!** (Henriette Anne Klauser)

Prager, again, from his book *Happiness Is A Serious Problem* thinks that the secret of happiness is gratitude; ungrateful people are never happy. The cancer survivor has a tremendous sense of gratitude. During the process of being grateful, you will only have positive thoughts in your mind. Nothing undermines gratitude as much as expectations, anticipations that things will turn out as *you* expect them to. Remember, *The Art of Living is really a continuous process of getting used to things we hadn't expected!* And that means today! And every day!

- ♦ **Beware of your expectations for they become your reality!** (Elita Darby)

Gratitude is dependent on getting what we don't expect. You should especially have limited expectations when you don't have control of the decision or situation, but as I'll point out later, you do have control of your *attitude!* The greater your expectations, the less gratitude you have if they come true, and no gratitude if they don't.

- ♦ **You don't have to say words to yourself to silently be grateful!**

The 'missing tile syndrome' that Prager describes is where you are confronted with a beautiful tile mural on the wall but with one of the tile missing, and all you can see is the missing tile. You expect perfection and when you don't see it, you are not grateful for the beauty of the masterpiece. Many people who might get a 98% correct on a test will only concentrate on the 2% they missed. Frustration builds on unmet expectations. Again, seeing only the missing tile engenders negative thoughts.

Many authors write of the problems generated by seeking only perfection. Rabbi Kushner makes a big point of this in his book *How Good Do We Have To Be?* He tells the story: "For years I was looking for the perfect man, and when I found him, it turned out he was looking for the perfect woman........and that wasn't me." Kushner goes on to state that we have to tell ourselves, *I am enough. Not perfect. Perfect wouldn't be good enough.*

True friendship is based on forgiveness—forgiveness and acceptance of imperfection in our friends, our loved ones and especially ourselves. McGraw, in his book *Self Matters. Creating Your Life from the Inside Out,* emphasizes what a lot of authors say about forgiveness: "Not until you can forgive, will you ever be free of anger, hate, bitterness and resentment. Up to this point you are the only one paying the price. It is your choice. It doesn't mean everything is OK or that the other person deserves to be forgiven. By forgiving, you suppress painful memories to outside your everyday awareness. But until you can forgive you can't grow or be happy." And remember,

Family, Friends, Fun, Fellowship, Faith, Forgive and Forget!

Kushner notes that withholding forgiveness may seem to give you a sense of power over someone, but you are the one who remains bitter and angry. The other person wins. Except many people thrive on their righteousness and anger—they suffer beautifully! *The act of forgiveness is an act of kindness towards yourself!*

You can <u>never</u> be happy by striving for perfection; excellence, yes, but not perfection. Keep in mind that even excellence is not self sustaining, you have to work at this. Striving for perfection can be self-defeating. *Don't keep doing the wrong thing better and better!*

- ♦ **By reducing our expectations, we reduce the amount of disappointment in our life!**

Learn to concentrate on what we do have rather than what is missing!

Some thoughts on being happier:

- The mere absence of any major problems at the moment should be a cause in and of itself for euphoria.
- Take a mental tour through a ghetto of Calcutta, a prison in a developing country, a children's cancer ward, a court dealing with child abuse, then ask yourself, "What's bothering me?"
- How would you feel if you lost everything you have right now and then got it all back?
- Laugh a lot!
- Never want to stop learning.
- If you have a disagreement or momentary mixed feelings about a loved one, how would you feel if he or she were suddenly gone forever?
- Be flexible on accepting change.
- Don't be a martyr.
- *Always believe the glass is half-full rather than half-empty.*

♦ **All the money in the world cannot buy a dying man his breath— so what does that make today worth?** (Og Mandino)

- The Dalai Lama recommends completing in writing 5 times, "I am glad I am not....," and do this for several things. Don't just think it, write it down! Another exercise is to write out is a worse case scenario of something that never happened to you like growing up in a third world country (see section on Write-Therapy).
- At bedtime ask your child what was the happiest thing that happened to them today. Write some of these down in their journal.

For some reason of human nature, we, as a society, have allowed negative thinking to override everything else, and that's because we have hard wired our brains into negativity. It seems to come automatically, being reinforced by the news events of the day (the media makes a living off of bad news), by our worrying. More on this in the discussion of attitude.

♦ **When bloated bureaucracies can't find victims that need help, they often create them!**

Talk to yourself. Tell yourself many times during the day that you intend to be happy, or tell yourself that you are happy and why. Smile while doing this!

Unhappiness

- The most miserable people are those obsessed with themselves. This leads to boredom and loneliness, with boredom being one of the most common and yet under recognized causes of unhappiness. They probably don't have real close friends. They become more materialistic, self-indulgent, and indifferent to others.
- I've noticed that unhappy people are worse tippers than happy people, who appreciate the service they've received.
- You can only have one thought at a time; it can't be both positive and negative. It's your choice. You become what you think. *Perception is reality.*
- You have no more right to consume happiness without producing it yourself.
- You will never be happy when you only see the bad in others.
- The negative person will be negative even in paradise!

♦ **Many people are unhappy about being unhappy!** (Viktor E Frankl)

- Preoccupation and obsession for what you don't have will never allow you to obtain joy and happiness, to enjoy the moment. This is wishing for things to be different. Wishing is a waste of your time.
- It can be the result of excessive expectations, especially of yourself—a perfectionist. Ask yourself, "What happens if I don't do this perfectly?" In a few weeks, you'll have forgotten you didn't do it perfectly and maybe begin to break the habit of perfection. Think positive!
- If you have the victim-mentality and blame others for your unhappiness, you will only perpetuate your misery and suffering through persistent negative thinking. The complaining person never complains about themselves. After a while, they believe everything they complain about. Don't make excuses—you alone are responsible for your happiness, no one else is.
- If we cannot find contentment in ourselves, it is useless to seek it elsewhere.
- Would rather be right than happy.
- Unhappy people tend to be attracted to other unhappy people! You should avoid these people.
- Unhappy people look older than they are, and they are more prone to illnesses!

♦ **Your peace of mind and happiness are with you now, not tomorrow!**

If you think you've had a bad day, ask yourself some of these questions as printed in an Ann Lander's column:

> Did a family member of close friend die today?
> Did you find out today that you have cancer?
> Did you lose your job?
> Did your spouse announce that he or she is leaving you?
> Did your daughter call from college to say she is married?
> Did you get shot at?
> Did your husband abuse you today?
> Did you find out your teenage son is an alcoholic?

There are dozens more scenarios you could come up with. Make a list of as many as you can and at night before you go to bed, check off all those that didn't happen! Be thankful for what you escaped—write this down in your grateful journal.

On awakening don't start the day by thinking of all the day's problems. Try to wake up happy. SMILE (this can drive your bed partner nuts!).

Always have something fun to look forward to; as we get older, this becomes even more important as a contributor to today's happiness. *Celebrate!*

♦ **The secret of happiness is not doing what one likes to do, but in liking what one has to do!** (Sir James M. Barrie)

This is attitude, and it is a continuum of positive thinking. For many people, they've allowed negative thoughts to fill their minds every day, all day. *We are what we think.* (I've said this before and I'll be saying it again).

♦ **When I get what I want, I will be happy—one of the greatest deceptions of all time!**

**Today is the 1ˢᵗ day of eternity—
Do something!**

**There is no duty we underrate as much
As the duty of being happy!**
Robert Louis Stevenson

Something in us militates against genuine leisure!
Tom Feltenstein

That something is *guilt!* We don't think we deserve to be happy, especially if we physicians are caring for sick and dying patients. Why not? A happy physician is a better physician. Your patients will respect this. A psychiatrist once told me that it isn't love that makes the world go 'round, it's guilt!

From a Jewish friend

♦ **Jewish Alzheimer's—you forget everything but the guilt!**

**There has never been a documented case report
Of someone on their deathbed saying:
"Gee, I wish I had spent more time at the office!"**

Roger Bone was a prominent physician scientist and educator with over 400 publications who died at the age of 56 of metastatic renal cancer. In the few years before his untimely death he wrote extensively on what it felt like to be dying as well as other end of life issues. He said many things, but one thing he said which is interesting considering his many accomplishments, *The things that one does throughout one's life that seem so urgent, are most of the time not so important.*

♦ **Don't take yourself and your life too seriously, life isn't permanent!**

**It's tough doing nothing,
You never know when you're done!**

This isn't necessarily true. One sage said that you don't achieve inner peace until you can spend an entire day doing absolutely nothing, and not feel guilty. Try it. Begin slowly with a few hours and gradually expand it to a whole day of waking hours. Don't wear a wrist watch during this time. Ruth Fishel in her book *Precious Solitude* extols the virtue of quiet time alone every day. Quiet brings wisdom; it is a spiritual and biologic necessity.

Serenity and peace of mind can be more healing than medicines. The very word *tranquility* has a peaceful connotation.

♦ **We never reflect how pleasant it is to ask for nothing!** (Seneca)

With serenity and solitude, impulsiveness fades. It is knowing that *I already have what I need.* You can't sense this feeling without noise-free time.

The greatest revelation is stillness!

During this time, think only peaceful thoughts, your blessings and never your problems. Regain the lost art of being alone. Loneliness expresses the pain of being alone, while solitude expresses the glory of being alone.

♦ **The right to be left alone—the most comprehensive of all rights and the right most valued by civilized man!** (Justice Louis Brandeis)

♦ **Start slow and taper off!**

♦ **There is more to life than increasing its speed!**

♦ **Even if you win the rat race, you're still a rat!** (Lily Tomlin)

♦ **How beautiful it is to do nothing, then rest afterward!** (Spanish proverb)

**Only those who are able to
Relax can create,
And then ideas reach the mind
Like lightning!**
Cicero

**Millions seek immortality but
Don't know what to do with
Themselves on a rainy Sunday afternoon!**
CF Chesterfield

They're bored! I've mentioned this before. And boredom in the adult has nothing to do with having nothing to do. It means that the individual's mind is so full of thoughts, good and bad, positive and more often negative, about the past and tomorrow, that they are paralyzed with inaction, and, maybe depressed! They cling so tightly to the past that they can't embrace the present. They can't get started on anything, including a hobby. They don't know how to practice serious leisure. The more you can concentrate on your leisure activity, the more you will enjoy it. Boredom may be one of the greatest causes of unhappiness and depression. You can't be bored if you are in the presence of family and friends you care about.

♦ **The measure of a person is how they handle their time alone!**

Nadine Crenshaw says that we alleviate our inner boredom by inventing extravagant outer lives, filling our free hours with play that is indistinguishable from work. Frankl, as a psychiatrist, said that boredom is a greater problem than anxiety and distress. And loneliness can be even more distressing. Volunteering is a great reliever of boredom.

Your mind is too full of things to enjoy the moment. Free time can be more difficult to enjoy than work for many people! Stop! Smell the roses. Listen to a child laugh. What if we saw only in black and white? Did you ever look at a beautiful scene and appreciate it in 3 dimensions? Instead of the flat two? Leonardo Da Vinci would call this *sensory intelligence—seeing what you are seeing.* Think about this. Try it!

♦ **What if the stars came out only one night every 10 years. What a celebration that would be!**

♦ **The secret of success isn't your material possessions or the positions attained, it is being happy with what you have, and how you have affected the lives of others, especially childrens' lives, including your children and grandchildren. A hundred years from now, only the latter will be remembered, not how many papers you published, how much money you made, or the success achieved!**

♦ **Learn to want what you have!**

♦ **Freedom from desire leads to inward peace!** (Lao-Tzu)

Sleep deprivation has to play a major role in many people's stress and unhappiness, significantly contributing to emotional exhaustion, low stress tolerance, burnout, and maybe, even impairing the immune system. In fact, one study suggests that for every hour of sleep sacrificed, you feel 8% less happy! I'm not sure how anyone came up with this number, but lack of sleep certainly doesn't enhance happiness! There is also evidence that it can accelerate mental decline as we age. We all vary so much in the amount of sleep we need every night, only you know when you are or aren't sleep deprived. For some, even a few days or weeks of sleeping-in isn't usually sufficient to catch up. Exercise and the proper amount of sleep should be high priority to you.

♦ **The sustenance of our emotional life is the ability to experience pleasure!** (David W. Swanson)

Sloooow down! Hurrying has become a habit for many people. They're driving faster, running red lights, eating meals in minutes. Where are they going? What are the extra few minutes going to gain them? Hurrying doesn't stop when you get out of the car. I suspect 'hurry-endorphins' are continuing to be pumped. Try to enjoy each bite of food, each little bite of life!

♦ **The really happy guy is the person who can enjoy the scenery while stuck in a horrendous traffic jam!**

In the 'old days' if you missed the stage coach, you were content to wait 2 or more days for the next one. Now, we get upset if the longer line next to you at the check out counter moves faster than your line! If you are in a traffic jam or slow moving line, you have 2 choices: you can spend the next 5 minutes, or hour, being angry and resentful, or you can relax and work on your happiness and appreciation intentions. Review your blessings. Remember, *life is full of delays and interruptions.* Accept this!

Sometimes the only reason to be happy is
Because you are happy!

Various authors have described 'pseudohappiness' or 'happiness traps' as more possessions, a life of leisure, overcoming your weaknesses, financial security, pleasure. Pleasure can be a temporary mask for fear and anxiety.

Make a goal of being as happy as you can be, every day. You have to work at this but only by letting it come to you!

♦ **Success is getting what you want and happiness is wanting what you get!**

In the end, what affects life most deeply
Are things too simple to talk about!
Nell Blaine

VOLUNTEER

♦ **A free person is not just freedom to do what you want to do, but the opportunity to do what you _ought_ to do!** (Terry Carroll)

This is a great way to counter boredom as well as change your perspective on life. To young physicians I recommend volunteering in non medically related ways and doing things you can do with the family. I take my grandchildren to parks and pick up litter. It's a quiet time with them, you can do it any time you want; you'll never run out of something to do and you'll teach them something you can't do any other way. There are many other things you can do with the family—soup kitchens, meals on wheels, and so on. It always leaves the world a little bit better. _The best thing you have to give is yourself!_ You can't be an effective volunteer without a certain degree of basic happiness.

**It is one of the most beautiful compensations in life
That no man can sincerely try to help another
Without helping himself!
Ralph Waldo Emerson**

Volunteering develops compassion, improves your self-esteem, and creates a transient euphoria. And it is a great way of establishing trust. Writing a check for the charity(s) of your choice isn't the same as _giving_ your time and even your expertise without an anticipation of reward or recognition to those who are less fortunate than you. And it can do wonders for your happiness. The warmth of just giving money may last for only a short time and can be driven by guilt and what Foster and Hicks call 'insincere obligation'. I'm all for giving of this kind but it doesn't substitute for giving of yourself. Do both!

♦ **The gift of self-giving can be as simple as smiling!**

Smiling at a stranger is an act of volunteering. There is no downside to volunteering. Begin slowly. Only two hours a month is the equivalent of a full 24 hour day a year! _How you interact with others affects who you are._ What you give away reflects on your character. You can't volunteer in any way without an element of compassion in you that you may not have known you have, nor a degree of happiness that you didn't appreciate that you have—build on this!

♦ **Do something for someone who can never repay you!**

Not quite the same as volunteering but how well do you know your neighbors? Are you a part of the community? In the days before the automatic garage door openers, we had to get out of the car to open or close the garage door and at the same time say hello to a neighbor and carry on a short conversation. Now, we can go years without ever even meeting them! I feel that we have an obligation to be a part of and contribute to the well being of the community and neighborhood we live in, no matter how busy we are.

Suicide appears to be partly the result of 2 situations: ineffectiveness and disconnectedness and both of these relate to a low self-esteem. It seems to me that for those at risk for suicide that volunteering where one can contribute to and witness the betterment of the lives he has helped would be therapeutic.

♦ **You volunteer because you care, not because you have to care!**

To truly love your country, you must begin with local civic pride which requires involvement. The health and vitality of any community is dependent on how well everyone in it treats each other. You can't do this sitting in your home. Have you ever missed voting? –don't!

♦ **We all want to do well, but if we do not also do good, then doing well isn't enough!** (Anne Quinlan)

> **The biggest disease today is not leprosy or**
> **Tuberculosis, but rather the feeling**
> **Of being unwanted, uncared for**
> **And deserted by everybody!**
>
> **Mother Teresa**

QUALITIES OF THE RESPECTED PERSON

There are a number of qualities a physician must have in order to practice the Art of Medicine, and as far as I'm concerned, these must be present in all physicians and should be *a goal of all people*, not just physicians. If physicians don't possess these qualities, or worse, don't want to possess these qualities, then they may ultimately be screened out by their patients, their peers, and the public. They should be present in the individuals applying to medical school, but I accept the fact that these can be honed and improved on with the maturing process of developing into a young physician under the tutelage of role models and mentors. But I am a strong believer that these <u>must</u> begin at home, starting well before the age of 3 years.

◆ **Life only gets better when you do!**

The table lists qualities I think are important not only in a physician but in every adult with one of the most important being the desire to improve in all areas, i.e., the motivation for continuous personal improvement. Your children's future happiness and success will depend on this. These are values of principles, deep fundamental truths, we live our life around. It is not meant to be all inclusive nor in any special order of importance.

> **Character**
> > **Integrity**
> > > **Trustworthiness. honesty**
> > > > **Attitude, an intent to be happy; optimism**
> > > > > **Humanism= empathy, caring, compassion, kindness**
> > > > > **Intuition, and acting on it**
> > > > > **Equanimity; resilience**
> > > > > **Lack of arrogance (humility)**
> > > > > **Communication skills and desire to use them**
> > > > > **Consistency, reliability, dependability**
> > > > > **Self recognition as a positive role model**
> > > > > **Spiritual acceptance**
> > > > > **Collegiality, nice person, composed, mature**
> > > > > **Knowing that you don't know (wisdom)**
> > > > > **People skills (emotional intelligence)**
> > > > > **Respect, for yourself, for others, for**
> > > > > > **diversity (tolerance)**
> > > > > **Balanced life, love of family, a passion for life**
> > > > > **Punctuality**
> > > > > **Loyalty/pride**
> > > > > **Professionalism**

Character is what you are. Not what you pretend to be to yourself or others. It is what you do over the years when you think no one is watching you. Or, *What you would do if you knew you would never be found out*. It is the totality of what you are, your thoughts, your words, and especially your behavior. It is living by quiet example. It communicates you. Don't confuse personality with character. Character complements honor and integrity and are gifts you give yourself. It is a consistency of all the other good qualities you have, especially a positive attitude, your integrity. *Someone of character has respect for those who can be of no possible value to him or her*. Choosing not to respond to a criticism about you shows character. Only you can damage your character.

- **Talent develops in quiet, alone; character is sharpened in the torrent of the world!** (Goethe)

**Watch your thoughts because they become your words
Watch your words because they become your actions
Watch your actions, because they become your habits
Watch your habits, because they become your character
Watch your character because it becomes your
Reputation!
Frank Outlaw**

- **Of all the properties of honorable men, not one is as highly prized as that of character!** (Henry Clay)

Character is a journey, not a destination. It is formed through relationships. It builds on personally learning how to deal with setbacks and challenges we all have, and to accept responsibility; this is resilience. Morally accountable character over a long period leads to one's reputation. *A reputation takes years to build, but it can be lost overnight!*

- **Character is higher than intellect!** (Ralph Waldo Emerson)

- **People hear what you say, but more importantly, they see what you do; and seeing is believing!** (Baggett)

Perception is reality. Reality is in perception. *We are what we do! What we think!*

- **Hire for character; you can train for skills and competence!**

Integrity is inherent in character; you can't develop true character without practicing integrity; it guarantees all other qualities and values. It is a firm adherence to a code of moral values, an implicit obedience to the dictates of your conscience, and is the ultimate test by which you measure one's character. Integrity is what you do every day whereas character is a long-term quality. There now seem to be fewer penalties for not having integrity, but that shouldn't demean its importance.

- **We are what we repeatedly do. Excellence, then, is not an act, but a habit!** (Aristotle)

The person of integrity doesn't have personal hidden agendas.

- **Character, integrity and wisdom are more important than knowledge and competence!**

**Integrity is treating everyone,
Including yourself, the same!**

This is respect. If you always do the right thing, you don't have to worry about making decisions. It is a parallel to the old adage, *If you always tell the truth, you don't have to remember what you said and to who!*

44

- **Truth is the one thing you can do nothing about!**

- **Integrity is a sense of one's obligations!**

Stephen Covey in his book *First Things First* points out that if you don't respond to your integrity, your intuition, you begin to build a wall around your conscience that reduces your sensitivity and receptivity to doing the right thing. He goes on to say, "As we make and keep commitments, even small ones, we begin to establish an inner integrity that gives us the awareness of self-control and the courage and strength to accept more of the responsibility for our own lives. Little by little, *our honor becomes greater than our moods.*"

- **I haven't committed a crime. What I did was fail to comply with the law!** (a major politician answering accusations that he failed to pay taxes!)

- **Wisdom is knowing what path to take; integrity is taking it!**

Integrity is the foundation of all lasting relationships. Everyone is comfortable with someone of integrity. It is the basis for your confidence in yourself and the confidence you inspire in others.

- **It isn't cheating if you don't get caught!** (high school student)

Integrity is doing what you said you would do,
When you said you would do it,
And how you said you would do it
And you can count on it!

It can be as simple as returning phone calls and e-mails, as being on time. Your word, your truthful word, can be a powerful force to those who receive it, and to yourself as you talk to yourself. *One thing you can give and still keep is your word.* Someone of integrity doesn't gossip—this is an attempt to boost your own self-esteem while putting someone else down.

Humility is said to be one of the greatest virtues, and is a constant companion of integrity; from this you can understand how the arrogant person might compromise integrity. The person of integrity fully accepts responsibility for his own actions and decisions, and doesn't look to blame others. Don't make promises you can't keep.

- **I don't know how she heard about your secret; everyone I told swore they wouldn't tell anyone!**

Resolve to be tender with the young,
Compassionate with the aged,
Sympathetic with the striving, and
Tolerant of the weak and the wrong.
Sometime in your life you will have been all of these!
Lloyd Shearer

Trust in their physician to many patients is more important in the choice of their physician than compassion, integrity and other virtues and is one of the main reasons for switching to another physician. However, the public has lost trust in the health care system and the personal trust in their physician is eroding right behind it. This is a sacred trust we're talking about, something as intangible as the art of medicine but integral to it.

♦ **If you can't trust your physician, who can you trust!**

Trust and honesty are necessary in every successful relationship in life. It is the glue of all human bonding and when you think about it, it is the strength of mutual bonding between humans and their pets. The patient's trust in their physician is an unquestioning belief that he or she will do what is best for them, without compromise, and that he or she is always honest with them, not hiding facts from them to protect the HMOs. Even if the outcome isn't as satisfactory as might have been hoped for, it doesn't diminish the trust for the physician because the patient knows (is confident) he or she did his best. The patient is satisfied, which is an outcome measure of trust; he feels that he has been managed fairly.

♦ **A man is not honest, simply because he never had a chance to steal!**
(Tom Feltenstein)

Trust also plays a significant role in end of life issues. If the patient doesn't have complete trust in his physician, then he won't be as likely to trust that the physician will do what he thinks is in his best interest, or tell him everything. And as a result, more often than not, the patient will take more of the decision out of the physician's hands, usually wanting more, rather than less be done because of the uncertainty of what his physician will do.

Satisfied patients are more compliant, acceptable to less personal control but more involved in decision making, more likely to disclose important medical information, and have less demand for more testing and/or referrals. Establishing trust has also been shown that the patient has shorter hospital stays, requires less pain medication, more likely to follow their physician's advice, and overall, is less costly to the health care system.

The trustworthy physician likely has all the qualities discussed in this section, that is, the physician practices the art of medicine including the Platinum Rule of Medicine. Honesty is foremost in the relationship. Proper communication is paramount as is compassion, competence and lack of perceived conflict of interest.

♦ **Listening builds trust!**

Greed can insidiously distort the physician's rational thinking beyond his imagination. Greed begets more greed and can become an addiction. And once greed for money becomes a way of life, it becomes easier every time a decision needs to be made on whether or not to do a procedure or order another test that might benefit him (the physician). It ultimately compromises trust, integrity, honesty and will destroy the person.

♦ **To be trusted, it is said, is greater than to be loved!** (Stephen Covey)

Establishing trust is an ongoing process; it begins with the first visit and is enhanced by congruence, which is actions consistent with a person's word. A negative first impression of the physician makes it harder, if not nearly impossible, to ultimately establish trust to its fullest extent. If the patient is bounced around among physicians, no trust can be established—there is no continuity of care. It is very disheartening to a patient who can't see the physician they were beginning to bond with, even if it was only one visit. The patient sees no commitment on the part of the physician or the system. However, many patients are willing to have preconceived trust in a reputable institution or group practice, even before they see their first doctor there. It is up to the institution (the physician[s]) to lose the trust.

Almost as important as the trust of the patient for the physician is reciprocal trust of the physician for the patient. This is especially true for the patient with a chronic illness. If the physician can't trust the patient to be compliant and involved in their own health care, he or she will lose interest in caring for the patient. I don't think many patients appreciate this.

It needs to be made clear to the patient that they are a *partner* in dealing with their medical problems.

◆ **Never tell a lie...unless lying is one of your strong points!** (GW Plunkett)

Attitude is everything. It is your most priceless possession. A positive attitude is the one characteristic that all successful people have in common.

◆ **Attitude is the first thing anyone notices about you!**

◆ **Perception is reality!**

**The greatest discovery of my generation is that
A human being can alter his or her life by
Altering his attitude!**
William James

**Attitude to me is more important than facts, the past, than
Education, money, failures, successes, giftedness or
Skill, than what people think.
We are in charge of our attitudes!**

My Circle of Happiness begins with attitude—it has to. Through the functional MRI and PET scans of the brain we know that attitude resides predominantly in the amygdala, a walnut shaped portion of the primitive brain. This is the fear center that was prominent in our ancient ancestors. They had a lot to fear, fear of being attacked by an animal, a fear of not enough to eat, a fear of being killed by a warring tribe. Fear of not surviving gave way to anxiety and worry and negativity; to loneliness and to workaholism. And even in prosperous times it is a fear of not having enough of. The amygdala is more prominent in people with a negative attitude. It is hard-wired there by years of negative thinking.

Your attitude can be negative or positive, but <u>never</u> both at the same time. You have ¼th of a second to decide. It is totally up to you to decide which one. If an acquaintance walks in a room, and your thinking is normally hard wired to that of a negative attitude, then you will automatically think the things you don't like about that person. But by working on you attitude, you can gradually over 6 to 12 months or more, "rewire your thinking". And begin on completing your circle of happiness. Then, when that person comes in the room, you will only recall the nice things about the person!

Our thoughts and our mood are interchangeable. You will not have complete control over a low mood which we all get, but you do over your thoughts—never forget this!

♦ **Everything can be taken from a man but one thing: the last of the human freedoms—to choose one's attitude in any given set of circumstances!** (Viktor Frankl)

Thoughts are powerful things. A positive cheerful attitude is immediately picked up by all those around you. It shows by your behavior and actions and especially your body language what you are thinking or feeling. Even though an employer may not appreciate it, it is the first thing they look for in hiring someone. A consistency of a positive attitude, even during a bad day, brings an aura of calmness to those around you and conveys a sense of confidence, without arrogance. It reduces stress. *Interestingly, negative emotions trigger autonomic responses contributing to many unwanted symptoms, but positive ones don't.* The power of positive thinking!

Because of our evolution, our thoughts and emotions tend to be controlled by our negative impulses rather than our positive ones. This is why being miserable is easy, being happy is hard!

Patients greatly resent a negative attitude in their physician, even if he or she is effectively communicating with them. They can't tell much about your character or integrity at the first visit but they sure can sense your attitude, and that leaves a lasting impression. Positive thoughts beget positive behavior. *Your mind will give back exactly what you put in it!* And keep in mind that your subconscious is working 24 hours a day! Delaying decisions and problems you go to bed with ("sleeping on it") are sometimes resolved by your subconscious overnight.

There are many things we have no control over, but we do our attitude. It is *the art of living in peace with that which we cannot change; the courage to change that which can be changed; and the wisdom to know the difference*, the serenity prayer. You can't be a positive role model without a positive attitude. This may take some effort and discipline but it can be done, and for the betterment of the profession, it must be done. Nothing is ever 100% ideal but a person complaining to anyone that will listen is a negative attitude that no one likes to be around. Complaining becomes a habit and reflects on your self-image and on the image others have of you. You become part of the 'blame mentality'. A negative attitude, negative thinking, reflects fear, anger, disrespect, a low self-esteem. It permeates the atmosphere.

♦ **There is nothing good or bad, but thinking makes it so!** (William Shakespeare)

A positive attitude is the result of the power of positive thinking. Norman Vincent Peale has sold tens of millions of books around this theme; and it works. In the near future it is possible that a form of PET scanning or MRI will become the formal lie-detector test, replacing the polygraph; it seems to be more sensitive and specific. The lie as created in the mind has produced a neurochemical pathway in the brain. So will a positive attitude. But it takes time, especially if it must overcome a built-up negative attitude in the brain neuropathways. It might take many months, or even a few years for some people and must be constantly worked on. *You can't allow old recurring negative thoughts to ever prevail.*

Positive attitude, the power of positive thinking, energizes the people around you. It is analogous to what exercise is to the muscles. Negative thinking and attitude has a similar analogy—they cause atrophy! Take charge of your thoughts. This requires discipline but well worth working at.

♦ **Retreat, hell! We're advancing in a different direction!**

One study showed that people with a positive attitude are luckier than those without it (some people seem to have too much time on their hands to be able to do these kinds of studies!). Positive emotions increases the likelihood that you will feel good later. Of concern is that grumpy people, people with a negative attitude, cost the US economy up to $300 Billion per year. Even if it is only a third of this it is an impressive statistic. Just a few people can produce a dysfunctional, inefficient work place. Add to this the cost of high employee turnover, work place injuries, absences and fraud, and you have something that almost demands some kind of action.

Back to the Circle of Happiness: The pneumonic ASKH serves as a reminder. As I stated earlier, it has to begin with a positive attitude that is followed by a smile (see Smile in the section on communication). A smile generates healthy endorphins not only in you but in the receiver. The more you smile, the more likely you are going to do acts of kindness which activates more endorphins and immunoglobulins. And all this leads to happiness with an improvement in self-esteem. You can't practice kindness without a positive attitude. Performing this circle re-hardwires your neural circuits while at the same time suppresses any negative thoughts. You will be a better person in all ways.

I think every employer should have at the top of the application form in large, bold print: **Don't bother to apply here if you have a negative attitude!**

There is the old story about 2 stone cutters. The first one was asked what he was doing and he said, "I'm cutting this big stone into blocks." The second one was asked what he was doing and he said, "I'm building a beautiful cathedral." *Which stone cutter attitude are you?* Are you building beautiful relationships? Or just passing the time of day, maybe making other peoples' day miserable?

♦ **Poise: the ability to keep talking while the other guy picks up the check!**

A positive attitude is not only contagious in your mind but also to the people around you, probably almost as infectious as kindness. And not only does it work now, but increases the likelihood that you will feel good later. Everyone, absolutely everyone has weaknesses; after you recognize this, work around them and capitalize on your strengths. Cultivate feelings of passion and excitement for life; you can't do this if you are hardwired on the negative. Believe good things will happen to you. From Ann Landers on the difference between *winners* and *whiners:*

> The whiner says, *I don't know and I'm sure nobody else knows either.*
> The winner says, *Let's find out.*
> When the whiner makes a mistake, he says, *It isn't my fault.*
> The winner says, *I'm responsible, and I'm going to see what can be done to set things right and to learn from it.*
> When a winner makes a commitment, he or she honors it.
> When a whiner makes a promise, he keeps it if he doesn't find something better to do, or change his mind.
> A winner feels responsible for more than his job calls for.
> A whiner says, *That's not my department.*
> A winner says, *There ought to be a better way to do it.*
> A whiner says, *That's the way it's always done. Why change?*
> A winner says, *I could be a lot better, and I'm going to try to improve.*
> The whiner says, *I'm not as bad as a lot of other people.*

To try to be better, is to be better
Charlotte Cushman

Empathy/humanism/compassion/kindness is half way around the Circle of Happiness and is the foundation of the physician-patient interaction but it is the first thing to go as medicine becomes more of a contract rather than a covenant. How can there be empathy when the patient sees a different physician at each visit? When greed and the bottom line becomes more important than anything else?

Smiling is the 2nd portion of my Circle of Happiness because you can't be kind without smiling. As you'll see in my section on communication, a smile can be one of your most important assets, providing you want to smile. Every morning on awakening, practice starting the day with a smile and put a genuine smile on your face as often as possible. You'll begin to notice that many people never smile while others always have a beautiful smile. The act of smiling makes you want to practice kindness. Thinking kind thoughts and performing acts of kindness will almost always lead to increased happiness (and smiling) whether you want it or not! Studies show that someone receiving an act of kindness is more likely to be kind and express kindness more than before the act. And it has been shown that the physician practicing kindness enjoys more professional satisfaction.

Kindness and compassion are the 3rd portion of my Circle of Happiness; that is what this section is about.

Empathy is the capacity to imagine oneself in the patient's world and to try to understand it, to try to feel what the patient feels. It is almost a transference of emotions. It is the ability to recognize unsaid emotions and encourage the patient or friend who is seeking solace to discuss them, but this can't be done without mutual trust. *Compassion is an attitude of wishing for others to be free of suffering; it isn't passive.* There should be some attempt to do something about the suffering, if indeed, the physician or you want to help. It is also the ability to see the good in others.

- **Compassion for yourself is the most powerful healer of all!** (Theodore Isaac Rubin)

Sympathizing is one step up—it is a desire to help, to alleviate. But not to pity.

- **Feelings (emotions) are both nouns and verbs!**

First seek to understand. It is almost as important to acknowledge that you are beginning to understand what the patient is feeling. If you can correctly read emotions, you'll likely react accordingly, at least by non verbal communication. Understanding is a key word; wanting to understand is the first step in compassion.

To better understand, listen beneath the words!

**I cannot begin to feel what you are feeling, but
You must know I care!**

You can let the patient know that you care, even without saying anything—they'll know. *Caring takes away the loneliness of suffering.* One argument given is that physicians don't have the time for empathy; however, in the long run, empathy may save time by the trust it builds.

**Sensitivity:
He takes a bath once a month whether he needs it or not!**

A simple statement of reassurance isn't the same thing as empathy and understanding. It cannot take the place of listening and communicating. You can't reassure unless you've established some trust with the patient, otherwise, the patient may wonder if you, the physician, really understands what is going on. They will see through over-reassurance. Over-reassurance is promising something you may have no control over.

- **Be kind. Everyone you meet is fighting a battle!** (Plato)

Unfortunately, empathy and compassion for the patient cannot be taught, it *must* be learned from role models. A negative role model should not be tolerated in a practice or academic center. They create a milieu that is counterproductive and destructive. It promotes disloyalty and can contaminate a whole culture.

It's OK for the physician to feel sadness (and to cry), as sadness is important to the development of compassion.

- **You can see farther through a tear than you can through a telescope!** (Lord Byron)

Empathy and compassion begin on the physician's part by the desire to care, a 'caring attitude'. You can care for someone you just met, before you have had time to develop an empathetic relationship, even if you don't know anything about them. Francis

Peabody said it best in 1927; he wrote a very lengthy article on caring for the patient and summarized it in the last sentence by saying:

The secret of caring for the patient
Is to care for the patient!

Empathy cannot occur without acts of **kindness** to everyone around you including yourself. It's a reassurance that we are not in this alone, that there are people that care about each other. Like family, friends and our home, kindness is a safe haven in a hostile world. Even the blind and the deaf can see and hear kindness. Practicing it begets more kindness and leads to a peace of mind and a sense of self-worth. It is a great tranquilizer. Even the smallest act of a kindness contributes to the whole. But the opposite is not true—a little act of unkindness should <u>not</u> take away from the whole. On the contrary, forget it; it's their problem. And kindness builds hope for the future, creating joyful but realistic expectations. *You cannot have tolerance without empathy and understanding.*

IT'S FUN TO BE KIND!

Kindness is both an attitude and an action. Kindness, like a smile, is universal language. It is not the rare big acts of kindness that bring happiness, it is the ongoing summation of many multiple very little acts of kindness that does. This is the ***butterfly effect.***

The butterfly effect is a famous epithet in the meteorology world. In 1960 while at a world climatologic conference Dr Edward Lorenz was discussing the effects of chaos and was asked, "Would a butterfly flapping its wings affect the weather 1000 miles away?" You can argue either way—no one can prove you right or wrong. But, I think the Butterfly Effect is one strong explanation for Mayo's 100+ years of success as I'll explain in the section on the Mayo Culture of Caring.

Kindness is synonymous with *mutual respect*, including kindness to yourself.

True kindness can't be given away,
It can only be shared!
Rabbi Harold Kushner

By performing acts of kindness, we give ourselves opportunities to be better persons. When you bring happiness to someone else, you should delve on it, think about it when falling asleep that night. It's self-esteem building, as per the Circle of Happiness.

♦ **When you are kind to others, it not only changes you—it changes the world!** (Rabbi Harold Kushner)

This is the butterfly effect, again. Can you begin to see now how it may influence a working culture such as the Mayo Clinic?

♦ **The nicest feeling in the world is when you do a good deed anonymously and someone finds out about it!** (Oscar Wilde)

Sharing someone's joy is an act of kindness, just as sharing his sorrow.

Today, make a point to compliment someone (genuinely) and acknowledge the kindness of others. This is essential for happiness. It's an act of appreciation.

> ◆ **Kindness is like pornography—you don't have to define it, you know it when you see it (or don't see it)!**

Intuition is 'attunement to information not otherwise perceived by the conscious mind;' it is insight, providing you are open to listening to your intuition. It can also be described as 'an act of coming to direct knowledge or certainty without reasoning or inferring.' It is inherently good, allowing the individual to know right from wrong. For this reason it is important for the physician to rely on his intuition as it almost permits a 'divine empathy' that gives insight into reality. This gives you a connectedness, a bonding into the patient's suffering. Some would refer to this as a mutual transference. This empathy is the foundation of the physician-patient relationship and greatly enhances the trust necessary. Mindfulness makes us more receptive to intuition. The greater your self-esteem and your peace of mind, the more you can trust your intuition. Intuition is an intrinsic system of ethics and should be a sixth sense. Trust it!

> ◆ **If you don't listen to yourself** (intuition), **it's unlikely that anyone else will!** (MP Nichols)

Unfortunately, many people, including physicians, have suppressed acting on their intuition as it will compromise their avarice, their ego. Integrity develops on discerning right from wrong, then acting accordingly.

Equanimity, a calm patience, an inner strength. Contentment. An imperturbability. In Osler's address on *Aequanimitas* he said, *In the physician or surgeon no quality takes rank with imperturbability...it is an essential bodily virtue.* I agree, it is truly an attitude and I think one of the virtues that an individual can master. Equanimity is an absence of anger, a peace of mind. A serenity. With peace and calmness of mind, you can much more effectively deal with setbacks. Wisdom is the fruit of equanimity.

> ◆ **What wisdom can you find that is greater than kindness!** (Jean Jacques Rousseau)

Osler's description of equanimity continues:...*means a coolness and presence of mind in all circumstances, a calmness amid storm, a clearness in* judgment..., in moments of stress and chaos. The physician without equanimity...*loses rapidly the confidence of his patients. It has the nature of a divine gift...a comfort to all who come in contact with him, whose example, I trust, made a deep impression* (the role model!). He goes on to point out that a good-natured equanimity is...*not to expect too much of the people amongst whom you dwell.*

He mentions that there is both a mental and physical component to equanimity. It would seem that you begin by acting physically through your body language in a calm manner and at the same time work on a mental attitude of being 'calm, cool and collected'. You are in control. Talk to yourself. (Note, this is the third time I've mentioned this. It works. If necessary, make a list of what you want to talk to yourself about, reminding yourself in a very positive way, of all your good qualities, in the present tense, using the word "I".) You are saying your self-esteem can handle the ups and downs of the day and still maintain an even keel. Your inner peace is reflected in a calm body language that begets more serenity, and in turn a trust with the people around you including your patients. Equanimity requires mindfulness and a surrendering of unessential attachments.

♦ **Enlightenment is the quiet acceptance of what is!**

It wasn't until later in my career that I realized that most of my role models and the people I respected the most had an equanimity about them and that was one of the reasons I respected them so much. Osler was right.

Stress is a challenge to anyone's equanimity, their 'imperturbability'. Wisdom comes with equanimity. I'm a believer that the calmer the parent(s), the greater the maturity instilled in the children; they need a calm sea in the storms of life. In a consistent way. Equanimity is something the other virtues build on, leading to a maturity in judgment. Contentment discourages greed. *A sense of calmness brings joy!*

James Allen wrote extensively on the theme of 'you are what you think;' he also was a believer of serenity. He said *...calmness of mind is one of the beautiful jewels of wisdom and is a result of long and patient effort in self control. The calm man, having learned how to govern himself, knows how to adapt to others. And not to expect too much of others. The more tranquil a man becomes, the greater his success.* I would add that serenity brings a greater respect for the person with this virtue by others as well as for himself. Anger is an outpouring of a feeling of inferiority, a sense of loss of control, a loss of self-respect.

Resilience is a coping mechanism. It is the response of an individual to an adverse situation. President Bill Clinton is one of the most resilient individuals that I know of; problems seemed to bounce off of him and he would come out smiling. It is a physical and mental hardiness that allows you to keep doing what you were planning to do whereas, lack of resilience derails you for varying periods of time and can aggravate or even cause a depression. If your brain is hard-wired in the positive at the time of a set-backs, you will have more reserve to deal with them.

We will all encounter many difficult situations in our lifetimes. Some are forms of rejection and everyone will experience these many times during their life. Use each one to your advantage—learn from them. Almost certainly 100% of the very successful people will tell you that they had major set-backs on their way up the ladder and it was what they learned from these that allowed them to keep climbing.

Anticipating these set-backs and writing out what is the best way for you to handle them is a reasonable alternative to stewing over them in silence. Invoke the *time factor*—what difference will the event make on tomorrow, next week, next month, ten years from now? Be kind to yourself. Remember, *This too, shall pass.* Write this on a card and carry it with you and look at it frequently when dealing with set-backs. And also remember this—what you do for others will be remembered more than anything else.

Patience is equanimity; it is the glue that holds society together by generating civility, an aura of calmness, control. Your children need to learn this from you. There is still a place for counting to ten.

♦ **Patience—eventually grass becomes milk!**

There is no place for **arrogance** in medicine. The opposite of arrogance is humility, unpretentious, yet the very humble or too humble person might be perceived as not in control or of low self esteem. It is my view that the public views arrogance in the physician as an even greater sin than greed and I think the problem is increasing in spite of the fact that the physician knows that poll after poll shows the stature of the physician has greatly diminished in the eyes of the public. We were once on top; now we're somewhere towards the middle of ratings of professionals. I believe much of this is because of arrogance, and not just the problems brought on by third party payers, patient expectations, etc.

Arrogance is an 'aura of infallibility,' a 'genuine or assumed feeling of superiority.' The arrogant person presents him or herself in an overbearing manner or cocky attitude. He is 'always right' (in my experience women physicians are far less likely to be arrogant than men), and you are to never question his authority. For this reason, you, the patient, don't need to ask him any questions, as he has told you all that you need to know!

♦ **Arrogance is the weak man's imitation of strength!**

This arrogant physician never has to say, "I'm sorry" because he has nothing to be sorry about! And doesn't have to say, "I don't know," or say or imply, "I care about you."

There is no such thing as a compassionate or caring arrogant physician. Physicians many times cannot or will not take time to care and express empathy, on the excuse of time constraints, and for this reason are possibly wrongly perceived as arrogant, an unfortunate compromise. The respected physician always finds time to care for the patient and the family. Even a mild amount of arrogance is quickly perceived by the patient which significantly taints the bonding and trust necessary for a comfortable physician-patient relationship.

Harvey Mackay, the business writer, views arrogance as one of the deadliest of all human failings that can destroy a business. It costs 10 times as much to get a new customer as it does to keep an old one! And it takes weeks to get a new customer and seconds to lose one. It is easy for the arrogant person to rationalize his position, and most don't even recognize themselves as arrogant, and don't care when told they're arrogant—they are proud of it because it supports their misperception of self superiority.

The English describe a gentleman as
Someone who can play the bagpipes—
But doesn't!

The following are some characteristics about arrogance or the arrogant person:

- ♦ Uninterested in facts unknown to them
- ♦ They don't know that they don't know
- ♦ Not inclined to listen
- ♦ Easily angered when someone threatens or challenges his authority; he fears failure
- ♦ It begets more arrogance

- Probably of low self-esteem
- A one-man clique
- Enjoys testing its limits
- Succeeds, up to a point, through intimidation
- Lacks wisdom and maturity
- Selects poor subordinates, probably in an attempt to protect his turf
- Has little respect by his peers and actually becomes the butt of jokes
- Self-encourages stupidity and doesn't learn from it, but works hard to cover it up
- See themselves as more important than the institution or the culture or the company
- Generally disrespectful of support personnel and younger peers, and in turn, receives very little respect from them
- Unappreciative. Lacks gratitude.
- It allows the individual to perform up to the level of his capabilities, but not beyond. And this has nothing to do with IQ but it does with emotional intelligence
- Low level of tolerance as well as poor acceptance of cultural diversity
- Lacks a sense of humor and certainly can't laugh at himself

I looked up arrogance in the DSM-IV (Diagnostic and Statistical Manual of Mental Disorders) and it isn't listed in the index. I would think the arrogant person lacks some social intelligence, otherwise, how could he not step back occasionally and see how others perceive him in such an unfavorable light! A good example of immaturity.

Self questioning, a self-reflection, as mentioned in the section on mindfulness, tends to protect a person from arrogance while at the same time promotes humility and self confidence—he knows when he doesn't know and is willing to learn.

I'm not sure when arrogance develops in a person's life but the potential probably does early on. It usually isn't until this person reaches some milestones in his life and some position of authority that it surfaces. It is likely that the physician lacking in communication skills is a major contributor to the development of the difficult patient. Add arrogance to that and you've got an explosive chemistry. It would be interesting to see if a person becomes arrogant as a defensive measure because he lacks verbal and nonverbal communication abilities.

- **A little success can be more dangerous than an occasional failure!**
  (RA Lee)

Besides the typical arrogance of infallibility, there are two other kinds, almost as devastating, and they are self explanatory. They are the arrogance of blaming the patient when things don't go according to the patient's or the physician's expectations, and the arrogance of ignorance, causing the physician to become defensive. This may be becoming more common as the patient comes to the physician with a web site print-out of their disease, knowing more about the condition than the physician! The patient needs to appreciate that no physician, no matter how hard he or she studies, can keep up with the rapid advancement of science.

- **The first time I walked into a trophy shop, I said to myself, "This guy is good!"**

Dealing with an arrogant peer is not easy, especially since they have relatively little insight into the phenomenon. But it may become easier now that patient and peer review are on the horizon. The 'superior' to this person must deal with this head on, as this attitude is demoralizing to the people around them. It's possible the arrogant physician won't be able to make a living practicing clinical medicine without some help. It must be kept in mind that the 'superior' may be just as arrogant.

I advocate a 360 degree review of each physician dealing with patients every year. A 360 is a feedback of anonymous comments from many of the people including patients and those who work with the person, physicians included. This includes negative as well as positive comments. If this doesn't cause some self-reflection and improvement if there are negative comments, then harsher measures may be needed.

Consistency in maintaining all the qualities discussed here is extremely important and befits your character. Your *dependability, predictability, reliability and accountability* are qualities that allow the people you work with as well as your patients and your friends to know where you stand at all times. This engenders a trust, and very importantly in these days, is a stress reducing factor.

◆ **Nothing is ever gained without enthusiasm and persistence!**

It's probably not necessary to repeat this again, but a sense of humor is imperative.

Maturity and Wisdom. These qualities are not interchangeable. The mature person usually possesses some wisdom but I've known people who have more than average wisdom but sometimes act in an immature fashion. The dictionary doesn't give a clear definition of what I think the two mean. There is much overlap with the most of the qualities I've mention with wisdom and maturity and I'll refer to them again several times in this book as I think they are very important, even if hard to define.

I don't think you can 'learn' maturity and wisdom; their nidus must begin in early childhood in an environment of mature, emotionally intelligent parents who possess equanimity. I've read numerous references to both of these qualities to see if it is possible to acquire them later in life. I'm not sure, but by listing many of these, it may reveal some ideas on ways of working towards them.

Wisdom
- *Is your perspective on life as it is, not as you wish it to be.*
- *Knowing and accepting that life isn't fair.*
- *Is insight—seeing between the facts and not seeing what isn't there. Requires a calm mind, an equanimity.*
- *Knowing when silence is the best answer.*

◆ **It is better to be silent and considered a fool than to speak and remove all doubt!**

- *Recognizing the unspoken—insight, again.*
- *Knowing that assumptions aren't facts, knowing what we don't know but willing to find out.*
- *Willing to change your mind in presence of true facts.*

**We are drowning in knowledge but
Starving for wisdom!**

- *Wisdom is the application of knowledge, and more powerful than knowledge alone.*
- *The first step to wisdom is silence; the second is listening. Quiet solitude brings wisdom.*

**Wisdom is not saying anything when
You have nothing to say!**

- *It is knowing how to take a hint.*
- *Is self discipline.*
- *Not fooled easily.*
- *It is the quality that keeps you from getting into situations where you need it!*

**You can't have wisdom
Without compassion!**

Maturity
- *Is the ability to read other human beings, and the ability to make a decision based on what is needed as opposed to what you want.* **It is doing the right thing!**
- *If you can express your feelings and convictions while taking into consideration other peoples' concerns without offending them, this is maturity (Stephen Covey)*
- *Is the ability to do a job whether you are supervised or not, and finish it once it is started.* **Do more than expected of you!**
- *Accepting responsibility for your actions.*
- *Patience.*
- *Grateful.*
- *Nonjudgmental.*
- *Good manners, a gentleman, a lady. Grace under pressure!*

**When you get to the end-zone,
Act like you've been there before!**

- *Ability to gracefully accept a compliment.*
- *Uses kindness and discipline in equal measure.*
- *Not impulsive.*
- *Non self-serving.*
- *Flexible. Accepting the inevitable.*
- *Able to make a decision now and then living with it without regret.*
- *Reliable, keeps his word, punctual, self disciplined, consistent, resilient, balanced life*
- *Ability to face unpleasantness, frustration, set-backs, defeat, without complaining or collapse.*
- *Willingness to forgive*

**Empathetic joy—the ability to take
Pleasure in someone else's joy!**

- *Never plays the comparison game—people who play this game never tend to compare themselves to those with less!*
- **The ability to laugh at yourself!**
- *Admitting, "I could be wrong."*
- *Living one day at a time—mindfulness.*
- *Emotional intelligence.*
- *Refuses to accept mediocrity.*

Are you unleashing the power Of your mediocrity, again!

- *Know when not to save something—throw it or give it away! Better yet, not buying something you don't need.*

Wisdom and Maturity

- *It is the ability to every now and then to stand back outside your sphere of influence and seeing how you are impacting those around you.*
- *The ability to see things as they are, not as we wish them to be.*
- *Wisdom is knowing what is right. Maturity is how to act on it.*
- *The Serenity Prayer: Accepting the things we cannot change, the courage to change the things you can (maturity) and the wisdom to know the difference.*
- *Common sense.*
- *There is a fine line between delayed gratification and self-deprivation. Maturity is accepting that and wisdom is knowing where the line is.*
- *The ability to know what is important and to disregard everything else.*

♦ **You can't learn from your mistakes if you don't admit to making them!**

Immaturity

- *Are always victims: blaming others becomes a way of life. Begets more immaturity through self-pity, leading to anger and more blaming.*
- *Feels entitled.*

♦ **My wife was immature. I'd be at home in the bath and She'd come in and sink my boats!** (Woody Allen)

- *Society frequently rewards immaturity in the most visible people like pro athletes, politicians, movie stars.*
- *Unwilling to learn.*
- *Rude, arrogant, angry.*
- *Poor coping skills.*
- *Indecisive.*
- *Requires immediate self-gratification.*
- *A negative attitude.*

♦ **Intelligent people believe only half what they hear. Wise people know which half!** (Harvey Mackay)

Now you can see why it would be difficult to summarize the qualities of wisdom and maturity in a dictionary. If a young adult knows the descriptions of wisdom and maturity, I think it is possible to work towards achieving these through a positive attitude and meditation.

> ♦ **This above all: To thine ownself be true...thou canst not**
> **Then be false to any man!**
> **William Shakespeare**

Above all, it takes a certain courage to develop and especially to maintain these qualities. In too many situations there is almost a disincentive to being virtuous. It has become an accepted way of life to cheat, lie, blame, to lack compassion, mostly because of the breakdown of the family and lack of role models, but *virtue is still its own reward.*

Respect. The physician with all the qualities I have listed always respects his or her patients, the people he works with, even if he doesn't always agree with them, and his family. And he respects himself. Civility carries with it the essence of respect as well as that of courtesy, politeness and consideration of others. This is graciousness. Success will not mean much without this.

> ♦ **Let me not neglect any kindness, for I shall not pass this way again!**
> (Dale Carnegie)

A love of family and friends. I'm a firm believer that the formulation of the qualities I've discussed begin up through age 3 years. This is why the parents must take an active role in these years of growth in their children—remember, *Family, Friends, Fun.* Parenting is one of the toughest jobs there is. It takes work. *It is not a spectator sport!*

> ♦ **Children—they need so little from us but they need that little so**
> **much!** (Rabbi Harold Kushner)

Eating dinner together as family as often as you can is one of the most valuable acts of bonding you can do. And there should be laughter at these gatherings. It is not a time for disciplinary issues, nor should it be rushed. Ask your children thought provoking questions. A good meal in a calm environment provokes happiness.

And your spouse—remember her? Plan a real date at least once or twice a month. Don't allow your work to drain you emotionally—don't become *emotionally unavailable.* Let your spouse and your children ventilate—deal with it!

> **Is it true that some parents, on seeing their newborn child for**
> **The first time say, "What can I do to screw up**
> **This kid's life?"**

In a letter to Dear Abby, the writer poignantly describes far better than I can about your commitment to your family: *I too used to work a lot of hours, sometimes working two jobs just to have that 'extra cash.' It seemed important to make sure my kids had the best clothes, toys, went to the best schools—whatever. I wanted to drive a nicer car, have a nicer house, etc. There was always tomorrow for field trips or the park. We could wait until next year to take that family vacation. Now there is no tomorrow. My son died last year. He was only 14. I would live in a cardboard box for the rest of my life to be able to go to a football game or concert with him. I would take the bus every day if it meant we could hit golf balls in the back yard again.*

All you really have to do is love your children every day, tell them you love them, hold and hug them, read to them, care about them, <u>every</u> <u>day</u>.

♦ **What can we do to promote world peace? Go home and love your family!** (Mother Theresa)

**If I knew how great grandchildren would be,
I would have skipped the in between!**

Punctuality, being on time, in the business world (medicine is now a business, isn't it?) is considered the most underestimated virtue. This is on the premise that if you can always count on the person being on time, you can count on them for other things. This is integrity. It is respect for other people. *Punctuality is keeping a promise.*

♦ **I have always been a quarter of an hour before my time, and it has made a man of me!** (Horatio Nelson)

The punctual person tends to hold other values, your values, as important and the fact that he or she makes an effort to be on time implies that they are of the mindset to do their best at everything they try.

**I've noticed that the people who are late are often
So much jollier than the people who have to wait for them!
EV Lucas**

Loyalty to your institution, your workplace, its culture, is critical to maintaining its ideals. This is integral to your and the institution's integrity. You don't have to agree with everything but as long as you work there, you need to support its mission, its vision. If you can't, you should leave. The culture of an institution is shaped by the totality of each other's interactions.

Ha! Ha! Your end of the boat is sinking!

♦ **Being loyal to those not present is integrity. In doing so, we build trust of those who are present. When you defend those who are absent, you retain the trust of those present!** (Stephen Covey)

To have pride in an organization, be it a company, a health care center, a team, a volunteer organization, your country, you first must be loyal to it. It raises your self-esteem and makes you want to work more effectively, to be your best, to be a part of the team. This is pride.

Professionalism is a mind-think, an attitude of upholding what society thinks the members of the profession should be doing to advance the well-being of the members of society, even at the some-time sacrifice of the members of the profession. A professional "...attempts to master a complex body of knowledge and skills in the service of others in such a way to inspire confidence and trust, while putting this above personal financial gain." This implies a willingness to refer a patient for another opinion. Some form of professionalism is now being taught in most medical schools and residencies.

I think one of the qualities of the respected physician is to maintain the standards of the medical profession without compromise. No one would disagree that the patient (and the health of society) comes before everything else. However, medical professionalism is eroding, with possibly the greatest cause being greed—greed of money, power, position--to the disregard of the patient. Competition for the dollar has replaced cooperation. I hear of physicians reluctant to teach their specialty in fear that this new knowledge will stop referrals! Teaching and learning is an integral part of professionalism. Without it we won't advance.

> ♦ **Actually, I don't care about money but it calms my nerves!** (Joe Louis)

There are a number of buzz words that further describe professionalism and include pride, dedication, commitment, non self serving, sacrifice, self regulating, an appreciation of the value of human worth, humanism, uncompromising, life-long serving, public service, accountability, the holder of core health values........

The true professional strives to attain the qualities I've listed. The term professionalism means to 'speak out', to 'profess.' The true professional, as well as the society of physicians, makes his intentions of professionalism known to the public through dialogue, ensuring a proper place for its values and for the vulnerable people that he or she professes to protect, and at the same time makes known its responsibilities to regulate itself. It should be a stabilizing force within society, a group of people that through an unwritten moral commitment to the public can always be counted on as their advocates in relieving the suffering of man-kind. No other profession but that of the physician can do this.

Can professionalism be taught in medical school? I think you can talk about it but only the role model and the culture of the institution can truly teach it. If there are enough good role models and competent leadership, then the culture of the institution takes on an atmosphere of true professionalism. This can be infectious.

A relatively new term, deprofessionalism, explains some of the problems happening in medicine and means "...a long-term erosion of professional authority as a result of patients becoming more assertive, more demanding, less dependent on homeopathic medicine, and less trusting of physicians." I would add to this, "...a more litigious society."

> ♦ **Succeed at home first!**

Study your own behavior, your qualities. Write them down in your journal. I need to reemphasize here that your greater involvement with your family and friends, having fun, being happy does not take away or diminish the importance of your goals of being a professor, a leader, a CEO, the best you can and want to be. Through a balanced life style, pacing yourself through discipline, managing stress, being happy, you are more likely to accomplish your goals and be more satisfied with life. *Live a legend, leave a legend!*

Nothing endures but your qualities!
Walt Whitman

This is the best legacy you can leave!

TIME MANAGEMENT

We are given many blessings
But one of the greatest is *Time!*

Time isn't money, it's everything! It's the most important thing you can spend. Things are replaceable but time is not. Everyone has the same 24 hours in the day and many will try to take advantage of *your* time instead of theirs, while most of us use it inefficiently. Practicing time efficiency can make your life easier in all ways. In Light's book on *Making the Most of College: Students Speak Their Minds*, he points out 2 very important findings: 1) the majority of the students wanted and valued mentoring, and 2) the difference between students that prospered and those that floundered was time efficiency.

♦ **One of the great challenges in life is to decide what is important and then disregard everything else!**

Time management is learning to recognize the inconsequential and then ignoring it. *Don't major in minor things.* Important matters are usually more important than urgent matters (not, of course, the urgency of an acutely ill patient). Remember to say NO—*If you pick up one end of the stick, you pick up the whole stick!*

♦ **One of the greatest labor saving inventions of today is tomorrow**
(Harvey Mackay)

If you work 60 hours per week, 45 weeks per year and can save 5% through efficient use of your time, this will amount to 135 hours in a year, more than 2 work weeks a year of your life. This is called working smart. It is a form of continuous improvement but you usually can't do this alone, the team needs to help each other do this. If you don't work at it, it won't come automatically. It may require the guidance of a time management consultant. And there are many books on this. Keeping a time diary for 2 to 4 weeks can be enlightening.

He's like the guy driving around the countryside
Completely lost,
But happy because he is
Making good time!

We all know people like this. They're like brownian movement. For some of us the busier we are the more important we seem to ourselves. Exhaustion from working seems to be a trophy, a mark of real character, a virtue. A 'nobility in suffering' surfaces. For many work becomes truly addicting, with the same withdrawal symptoms as chemical addiction. *When work becomes its own reward, then it is no longer satisfying* and we work harder to try to get that 'high'.

But being a workaholic can be counter productive and certainly other aspects of your life will suffer. For many it is an escape from intimacy. The non workaholic can accomplish just as much 'work' by working smart, not longer hours. Long hours can be very counterproductive. It is important to work effectively while you're working— don't *waste time!* One of the greatest wastes of time is television. The average adult spends 4 hours a day watching TV. Television isn't for your entertainment, it is to sell you something. I have already mentioned the importance of balance in your life. As hard as I've tried, I cannot figure out how television in any way contributes to balance. I deal more with this in the section on stress.

**How did a fool and his money
Get together in the first place!**

♦ **Two-thirds of adults surveyed state that they would rather have
more time than money!**

**Auto mechanic: "I couldn't repair your brakes,
So I made your horn louder!"**

Steven Wright

MINDFULNESS

I would not have expected to include this subject in a discussion on the art of medicine, or for that matter, the art of living, but after reading several articles in medical journals and a few books on the subject, I realized how important it is for all of us, and not just physicians. Some medical schools are offering courses on it. It is one of the most important aspects of *working smart, of happiness.* You can't be appreciative or grateful without it.

> ♦ **Concentration is the secret to strength, perseverance and excellence!**

Mindfulness is a state of enhanced self awareness based on concentration and attention to the present moment. It is the ability to stand apart from ourselves and examine (by thinking) the results of our actions and to better understand how our mental status, motives, goals, emotions, habits, and bodily feelings at that moment, affect others. You can't be angry <u>and</u> mindful. Mindfulness requires a discipline, a certain attitude, and the ability to relax and enjoy the moment. Performed in the presence of another person such as the patient, brings about a sense of trust, a connectedness. It is done with eye contact and listening. The other person is quickly attuned to this, and just as quickly recognizes when it isn't present.

Other synonyms include 'openness,' a 'connectedness,' an 'intuitive or mindful state,' 'attunement to information not otherwise perceived by the conscious mind' (insight), 'non mindset,' 'living in the moment or the present,' 'the art of noticing' and 'listening to our feelings and conscience and acting appropriately on them' (intuition). It is being *fully present* to whomever you are conversing with while at the same time the ability to self-reflect (self-awareness) on how your own emotions relate to the interaction with the person you are with.

Living consciously is not stressful, a burden or time consuming, in fact, it is time efficient, while multitasking brings stress, inefficiency and mistakes.

> ♦ **Mindfulness is savoring the moment, no matter what is happening—you're alive! Makes you forget the problems of the past, the worries of the future! It is distraction resistant. It is singletasking. It takes great discipline to achieve maximal mindfulness!**

It is giving 100% of your thinking to what you are doing—playing, working, solitude, relaxing, family, friends.

**The physician must be mindful of himself before he
Can truly bring the capacity of mindfulness to those he serves!**

True mindfulness requires and contributes to good mental health on the part of the person practicing it, and in the patient-physician relationship, it greatly enhances trust as the patient can quickly sense when the physician is attuned to them. You have established rapport, and put the patient at ease. It requires a considerable degree of maturity, as it is necessary that *you see the world as it is than as you wish it to be.* And the more skilled you become at utilizing mindfulness, the more wisdom you acquire. But you have to consciously work at being mindful.

It is interesting to see how qualities I've mentioned so far all seem to be interchangeable with each other including mindfulness, and especially *wisdom, maturity, intuition, trust, attitude, compassion, lack of arrogance, a balanced life, thinking, respect for yourself and others you interact with, and professionalism.* Good *self-esteem*, as noted in the center of the Circle of Happiness is imperative to maximize mindfulness.

This seems to be a lot to consider but that is the point of this book—**being the best you can be through the desire to use continuous improvement of yourself!** I had no appreciation of the value of mindfulness when I started writing this book, and like so many other experiences of a teacher, the teacher probably learns more than the student(s).

Other terms that describe mindfulness: *attunement* to information not otherwise perceived. *Insight*, an interconnectedness between the physician and the knowledge he or she possesses that might relate to what the patient is telling him, is not the same as *intuition*. Intuition comes with experience and maturity. It requires an introspective processing of the information coming into your brain without judgment, expectations, preconceived notions, or an intolerance for the person in front of you, irrespective of your prejudices (the mature person, especially the physician, should have dealt with his prejudices before he got this far!).

♦ **Mindfulness requires compassion to see the patient as a person (humaneness) and not a disease!**

Probably 95% of what we do is out of habit, without the need to rise above the level of passive awareness; our actions and thoughts being on auto-pilot, going through the day in a mechanical fashion, not wanting to rock any boats.

♦ **The greatest mistake you can make in life is to be continually fearing you will make a mistake!** (Elbert Hubbard)

Mindfulness/living consciously requires a commitment, a discipline, an effort which many don't want because it will cause them to confront realities, including painful realities. However, these confrontations are necessary to strengthen our self-esteem and character. It is a necessary function to survive.

Many of us live in a world of daydreaming where our minds are carried along by our emotions at the moment, by mental associations. In this state of mind you don't have to deal with reality; you rationalize, blame, self-judge, clown around and see yourself as a victim. You live in a state of denial without passion. You aren't aware of the joy of the moment, except to place wishes above reality. These people frequently use misery as a teacher and build on this. The result of all this is a feeling of anxiety and frustration, encouraging even more fear of facing reality.

The more you live consciously, the more you will enjoy life, and the greater will be your **self-esteem**. It seems that mindfulness is essential for this. Branden, who has written extensively on self-esteem as well as *The Art of Living Consciously,* points out several features of self-esteem, including what I think may be the most important—it is the *self realization that we are worthy of happiness*. It reflects our deepest inner vision of ourselves, of our worth and competence.

♦ **We don't much deal in facts when we are contemplating ourselves!**
(Mark Twain)

Self-esteem is what you think and feel about yourself, it is your self-reputation. It is the confidence in your ability to think and cope with the basic challenges we all encounter in life. The more 'routine' challenges and choices we are faced with, the greater the need of good self-esteem. Someone with high self-esteem has a sense of control over his or her life and is self reliant, not needing to judge others because he doesn't need anything from them. They have an *emotional surplus* that allows them to care about others, in addition to themselves. A resilience.

♦ **The better I feel about myself, the more willing and able I am to help others!**

Being charitable by giving of yourself is an amazing boost of self-esteem!

High or low self-esteem tends to be associated with self-fulfilling prophecies. The best example of this is the child who is told he is no good and will never amount to anything. *Perception becomes reality.* Self-esteem develops in our earlier years and is nurtured by many role models (good and/or bad) in the formative years. Individuals with low self-esteem have feelings of worthlessness and inadequacy, lack of self-confidence and some tend to be arrogant as a defensive measure. They allow their material possessions to define who they are rather than their character. They become pre-occupied by hurts and perceived injustices. Pre-occupied is the buzz word here. *It is a free-floating negativity.*

♦ **My inferiority complex isn't as good as yours!**

Our self-image essentially determines what we become. It says, "I can," whereas pride says, "I did it."

Alcoholics Anonymous is one of the most successful self-esteem builders when nothing else has worked. Their *Just for Today* philosophy of life is worth repeating here as it summarizes in a few words what all of us, even those with high self-esteem, can live by:

Just For Today I will
- **Live this day only**
- **Be happy**
- **Strengthen my mind**
- **Accept what is and not try to change it**
- **Do a good turn**
- **Do 2 things I don't want to**
- **Not show my hurt if I have any**
- **Be agreeable and not find fault**
- **Be kind**
- **Have a plan for the day and not hurry**
- **Have a quiet 30 minutes to myself**
- **Be unafraid**

Talking to yourself about these goals can be reinforcing. Be positive, using the present tense. Describe to yourself your best attributes and build on these.

- **Nobody holds a good opinion of a man who has a low opinion of himself!** (Anthony Trollape)

Branden and others list other features associated with good self-esteem:

- Living consciously/mindful/aware
- Is respectful
- Doesn't seek or need approval of others
- Living purposefully and has developed a philosophy of life
- Trusts his intuition
- Willing to take risks
- Active positive *thinker*
- Resilient. Able to persevere. Flexible
- Able to laugh at him or herself
- Understands reality and able to face it including discomforting facts without emotional hang ups
- Poised, relaxed
- Comfortable with aloneness
- Not a procrastinator
- Personal integrity
- Realistic self-acceptance; able to love himself in spite of failures. Doesn't seek perfection
- Self-responsibility
- Self-assertive
- Decisive
- Able to tolerate interruptions, delays and disappointments
- Never harbors unresolved anger
- Ability to enjoy life, relax and have fun
- Committed to continuous learning
- Confident enough to accept when wrong and willing to change
- Able to forgive himself
- Being a friend is more important than having one

Many of these are a repetition of what has already been discussed but serves to point out the common themes and virtues of continuous self-improvement.

Miguel Ruiz in his book *The Four Agreements* lists the '4 agreements' we should live by that I think significantly contribute to a good self-esteem and they are 1) the words you say and stand by, 2) don't take anything personally, 3) don't make assumptions, and 4) always do your best. Doing your best because you want to, without any anticipation of reward over the long haul can significantly boost your self-esteem. And this leads to happiness. This requires *action*. Watching television is inaction. A negative attitude is a form of 'reverse action' that siphons away your energy and ability to be your best.

Ruiz goes on to say that our biggest fear is of being who we are and then go on trying to live by other people's expectations, of not being good enough. As a result we create in us an image of perfection that no one can live up to. And so, we develop a fear of rejection, by others as well as ourselves! You need to learn to say, *So what!*

Action itself increases our self-esteem, especially if we successfully do something we are apprehensive about or fear. It is the opposite of procrastination or apathy. Action is necessary if you are to rise above yourself, to grow, to change for the better. A non assertive person spends lots of energy avoiding conflicts, manipulating others with a passive-aggressive personality, minimizing responsibility and blaming others. By blaming others it gives you an excuse to fail, further eroding your self-esteem. Blame and low self-esteem lead to more negativity.

In spite of negative influences in a young individual's life, it is possible to raise a person's self-esteem. The desire and motivation must come from within. It can be done but it must be worked at, usually from supportive help of others. But keeping it there can be a problem. Chipping away at your integrity undermines your self-esteem. Young people including physicians facing new and difficult challenges, failures, exhausting hours and other stresses may find this especially true. Don't despair.

Once you realize that you are accountable for your problems, you will understand that the solutions lie within you.

Alice Potter discusses the importance of affirmations in her book *The Positive Thinkers 10 Commandments,* especially the need to use the word "I" in the presence tense, not future tense, such as, "I am the best writer," or "I am the best basketball player," and repeat these endlessly. Do this by talking to yourself. As I stated earlier, being positive in the Art of Living, the Art of Playing, the Art of Working requires a lot of work and determination.

> ♦ **Self-hate limits our responses to life, because we always have to be on the lookout for ways to protect our shaky self-esteem!** (Nadine Crenshaw)

Love yourself. Believe in yourself. Learn to never react emotionally to criticism. Analyze the situation as to whether or not it is justified. If it is, correct it. Otherwise, forget it. Don't let anyone else affect your attitude. Build on your integrity and your equanimity and it will come. Learn from your role models.

> **Pay no attention to what critics say; no Statue has ever been put up to a critic!**
> **Jean Sibellus**

To live mindfully, consciously, we are aware of reality, our mind is open to receive beyond what our senses tell us—we don't just see and hear. We absorb in depth the details presented to our senses and think, actually thinking and concentrating, about them. It is knowing what we are doing while we are doing it. Look at the waves in the water, listen to every word directed to you, note the smell and beauty of a flower. *If you can begin to appreciate the beauty of a single flower, you will begin to appreciate the meaning of life* (Buddha). Life becomes exciting if you can learn to concentrate on everything and everyone around you at the moment, narrowing it down as appropriate. This adds to high self-esteem.

> ♦ **Life can be a wonderment to those with a positive attitude!**

Become aware of your instincts. Many of the mistakes in life occur as a result of ignoring our feelings. Learn to know your feelings. If we were to be more mindfully aware of our body, we would be healthier. A good self-image of your body leads to healthier habits. Imaging or visualizing your goals can be a very effective way of successfully accomplishing anything. Write them down.

70

♦ **How can the person feel free to open up when I evaluate everything he says before he says it or explains it!** (Stephen Covey)

Multitasking is the gist of Carlson and Bailey's book on *Slowing Down to the Speed of Life* and to Branden's *Living Consciously*. We try to think of too many things at once and accomplish little. Multitasking can entrap us into negative thinking and encourages us to react in an habitual fashion as a way of dealing with too many things on our mind. Instead, we should be concentrating on being fully present with whatever is going on at the moment, what the patient is saying or telling you including through their nonverbal body language. You are able to put aside your own feelings and witness how the patient's illness is causing suffering and to empathize with them. This is compassion based on insight. By doing this you see the person as a patient, not a disease.

One of the arts of seeing,
Is to not see what isn't there!

You don't accept everything as fact. This becomes intuitive thinking, rather than assumptive thinking, as a way of discovering, but becomes suppressed when we go into the analytic mode of thinking, or are thinking of more than one thing at a time.

You have to be willing to admit you don't know when you don't know! This is wisdom. By doing this the patient senses that you are in control in trying to care for them and this can be very important in establishing trust. I've been impressed over the years how much a patient or even just a friend or acquaintance appreciate it when you say you don't know. Then you go on to say that you'll try to find out.

Carson and Bailey point out that analytic thinking is not mindfulness and that it is a major contributor to fatigue and stress. It creates deadlines which are one of the greatest causes of stress. As a result we feel rushed and we then make more mistakes. Analytic thinking allows unrealistic thoughts to prevail and it suppresses free-flow thinking—it takes us out of the moment. We're not working smarter or thinking clearer; we tend to react out of habit rather than acting on the data our mind is sorting out.

Not surprisingly those able to live in the present rather than in the past or the future are less likely to be depressed. You can't experience joy unless you live in the moment.

♦ **I have dealt with many crises in my life but few ever happened!** (Mark Twain)

With free-flow thinking, answers tend to come out of the blue rather than trying to force them out with analytic thinking; this can lead to 'divine inspiration.' It allows us to slow down, work smarter, but not harder or longer hours.

Mindfulness allows us to develop a 'social intelligence' or a social awareness which allows us to see ourselves as seen by others rather than misjudging ourselves with analytic thinking and constantly going over all our faults and mistakes by living in the past. We become aware of our effect, the impact of our actions, our values and goals on ourselves as well as on other people, both good and bad. Wisdom and maturity allows us to then adjust accordingly. If it is 'bad', then forgive yourself and learn from it. This enhances your self esteem and this 'image' is then recognized in your body language by those you are relating to. I think this is an extremely important component to social as well as emotional intelligence.

This social self-awareness promotes empathy on the part of the physician which is an absolute necessity in the patient-physician relationship; it is the bonding of an interpersonal trust.

Resilience is a form of mindfulness. It is a learning/coping mechanism versus the victim/blaming/anger response when encountering a setback. Resilience is a reaffirmation of your belief in yourself, your self-esteem. It diminishes your fear of rejection—remember what I said earlier about saying **"NO".** Some people know how to say 'No'; it isn't a rejection of you, just a self protection of themselves. Respect this. Every successful person has failed at one time (or, more likely, many times) and learned from it. Failure isn't a rejection, it is an opportunity.

This ability to be and to feel connected to others, and thus a way of coping when dealing with adverse situations, allows one to bounce back that much quicker. The resilient person has a physical hardiness and calmness, yet remains sensitive to people while the non resilient individual is easily excitable and irritable, and more self centered. It is felt that resilience can be learned through discipline and this is important to the physician who will encounter many disappointments during his or her practicing lifetime.

♦ **No one can make you feel inferior without your consent!** (Eleanor Roosevelt)

Constant analytic thinking (mindlessness) is frequently negative thinking and leads to obsessive thinking resulting in stress, frustration, boredom, depression, loss of control, inflexibility, and burnout. The mindless person develops habitual behavior patterns to minimize further outside influences on his life, and as a result loses independence. Life goes on while our thinking is somewhere else. All this often results in deviations in professionalism. The mindless person becomes unwilling to 'think outside of the box' because he is living in the past or the future, which is what I mentioned earlier, 'pretraumatic stress syndrome.' Stress, fatigue and sleep deprivation lead to further mindlessness. And if you are living only in the past and in the future, you can't be enjoying the present.

Unexamined emotions on the part of the physician will produce frustration and powerlessness when the patient's illness progresses resulting in a desire to avoid patients to escape these uncomfortable feelings.

♦ **I don't like people who remind me of myself!**

Most people fail to recognize that their feelings
Towards others are determined by their
Feelings towards themselves!

Sidney J Harris

THINK

The two most common
Substances in the universe:

Hydrogen
&
Stupidity

When I first came across this some years ago, I thought it was kind of novel, but since then I realize how commonly we all do stupid things, some much worse than others. Look at what some of our professional athletes, politicians, media personalities and others do! Stupidity has nothing to do with IQ.

Stress makes people do stupid things!

The trouble with stupidity is
You can't quit when you're ahead!

Rule of the hole:
When in a hole, stop digging!

To me the implications of stupidity are 1) we don't *think,* and 2) because we don't think, we don't learn from the stupid mistakes and go right back and do something stupid again, believing that the next time will bring better results! We get stuck on stupid. Anger always affects your emotional intelligence, sometimes to the stupid level! I'm convinced that watching sit-coms glorifies stupidity, making it 'acceptable!' Maybe in this situation stupidity becomes a stress reliever!

In Freeman and DeWolfs' book *The 10 Dumbest Mistakes Smart People Make and How to Avoid Them* they use the word *dumb* in place of what I've called stupid. All 10 of their mistakes have to do with *misguided thinking* rather than something specific like selecting the wrong stock to buy, or a wrong career choice. Making mistakes, doing stupid things, misinterpreting and misjudging people and things and events actually becomes a habit to many people. It's more than the fact that they don't think, they do think but in a reflex way. It is *unrealistic thinking* or what I refer to as *dysthinking;* they don't think in a real-world way. This has nothing to do with positive thinking or attitude, but positive thinking can overcome the poor habit of dysfunctional, reflex thinking. I call this 'assumptive thinking', relying on past knowledge which may be inaccurate, and assumes that others think as we do!

◆ **Stupidity....is cutting a hole in the bottom of the boat to let the water out!**

I'm listing the 10 mistakes that Freeman and DeWolf discuss in length because they succinctly describe what a lot of us do. Their very titles almost say it all.

1) <u>The chicken little syndrome</u>. Awfulizing. Is catastrophic thinking. Assuming the worst without questioning or challenging what is happening.
2) <u>Mind reading</u>. Making assumptions what the other person is thinking. Is actually a form of laziness. And more often than not you assume on the negative side of the thought. We make these assumptions because we

73

may not have the courage to ask questions. Living by assumptions leads to false expectations and this always leads to unhappiness.

3) Personalizing. Again, another form of possible false assumptions and frequently leads to hurt feelings. It is a waste of energy and can enhance anger. An enhanced self-esteem minimizes personalizing. You should be able to say, "So What!" Learn not to take anything personally; "It's their problem."

4) Believing your press agent, who, most often is you.

5) Believing your critics. Listen to your criticism to see if you can learn from it, but always question the source and if it is true.

6) Perfectionism. Accept the fact that nothing is perfect. Your life will be easier. Accepting anything but perfect leads to anxiety, guilt, frustration and stress.

7) Comparisonitis. We usually tend to compare ourselves to people we *think* have more than we do or who *seem* happier than we are. This falls under the category of unmet expectations and leads to unhappiness. Write out incidences of when you compare yourself to others and see what you are comparing (see Write-Therapy).

8) What-if thinking. One word can summarize this—*worry!* More unrealistic expectations and a lot of negative energy is expended on this and we don't usually delve on good what-ifs. Freeman and DeWold recommend scheduling a specific time of day to worry, if worrying appeals to you.

9) The imperative *should*. We're talking about guilt here.

10) Yes-Butism. Can't say "NO". Non assertive. Deflecting action. Laying blame.

All these mistakes are avoidable or at least can be minimized by not allowing emotional reflex thinking rather than stepping back and realistically and logically thinking out what is actually taking place at that moment—*mindfulness!* This requires good self-esteem, wisdom and maturity, and can definitely be accomplished by working on it. I've said it before and I'll say it again, we all make mistakes but we must learn from them and move on! *Mindlessness* leads to doing or saying stupid things.

The average adult spends <10 minutes a day thinking!

Thinking is not the recycling of the opinion
Of others, or spewing out memorized data.
For some it is just the rearranging of their prejudices
And their misinformed 'facts'!

When you stop and think about it, the mass of society spends 30 to 90 or more minutes a day commuting with music blasting in their ears, punching data into a computer, or performing a labor or service function, coming home, popping something in the microwave, watching 4 hours of sit-coms or all evening in front of the computer, going to bed and starting over the next morning without probably putting in more than 2 to 5 minutes actually thinking. They spend more time planning the social events for the weekend than what they are going to do with the rest of their life. Unfortunately, very few people are rewarded by the company for any thinking they might do.

**The great contribution we can make is to prepare
The oncoming generations to think that they
Can and will think for themselves!**
CH Mayo

**Instructions from teachers and books teach a man
What to think, but the great need is that
He should learn how to think!**
WJ Mayo

I think the fringe groups of people such as terrorists, militia and fanatics of any nature are of normal IQ but have lost (or never had) the desire to learn, to think for themselves. They've lost the beauty of reasoning. From early youth on they are told what they should know and what to believe and are not allowed to think. As a result they can never acquire wisdom. And they become even more brain-washed. They function on a perverted instinct of hate and probably spend less than 60 seconds a day in spontaneous individual thinking.

♦ **Learning without thinking is useless. Thinking without learning is dangerous!**

I don't know the best way to teach someone how to think, but as learned professionals we have an obligation to think about our patient's problems and ask ourselves, "What am I missing?", "What are they trying to tell me?", "Am I overlooking anything?" Errant assumptions brought about by being on auto-pilot lie at the root of many failures.

Thinking at the moment becomes a major component of working smart. This is *mindfulness.* Critical self questioning of all received data as to whether or not it is factual, without bias or prejudice, gives us insight into what we do and don't know. And this is wisdom! In your mind, always challenge the assumptions. *Assumptions are not necessarily facts!* Don't let your brain go on automatic. How you think about a problem can be more important than the problem itself.

**THINK! It's the hardest, most valuable task
Any person performs!**
Harvey Mackay

♦ **Some people approach every problem with an open mouth!** (Adlai Stevenson)

♦ **If you lose the power to laugh, you lose the power to think!**
(Clarence Darrow)

Many ideas come in short bursts of insight—be aware of these as they occur and don't let them pass without thinking about them and if necessary act on them. Write them down.

There are many reasons we 'dysthink' with the major ones being stress, low self-esteem, anger, illness, sleep deprivation, fatigue, just plain laziness and others. As you encounter the need to make decisions, you need to ask yourself if any of these are affecting your ability to think.

Stupidity got us into this mess….

Why can't it get us out!

EMOTIONAL/SOCIAL INTELLIGENCE

If you're not smarter than a lot of people,
Or a more gifted athlete than most,
You can always outwork them!
Porter Payne

80% of success is showing up!
Woody Allen

After reading numerous articles and comments on success, I think Woody Allen is right. Showing up does not entail brilliance, or long hours. Instead showing up means

> Dedication
> Persistence
> Commitment
> Loyalty
> Consistency
> Mindfulness/aware of the moment
> Working smart

> ♦ **I accept mediocrity, as long as it is done well!**

Only the mediocre person is always at his best!
Somerset Maugham

A few years ago in an NFL press release of the 5 former pro football players who were to be inducted into the Hall of Fame, it was stated in 4 of the summaries that "He missed only 3 games in 11 seasons," "...started in 177 of 178 games," "...played in 107 straight games," and so on. These 4 were inducted into the Hall of Fame not only because of their consistency, of course, but *they showed up!* I suspect that there were a number of their peers who were stronger, faster and smarter than they were, but the winners worked smarter, and they came to play, albeit with some luck that they didn't suffer from a serious injury. They wanted to play and they wanted to win. They had a passion for the game. All physicians should have such passion. We're also professionals!

> ♦ **I couldn't wait for success so I went ahead without it!** (Jonathan Winters)

How many work here?
About half do!

Carrying your share of the load, plus a little more is team work. Honing a proper work ethic is critical. *It doesn't take talent to hustle!*

> ♦ **Among the chief worries of today's executives is the large number of the unemployed still on the payroll!**

A genius can do just about anything...
Except make a living!

If you have a choice of being

NICE

Or, being

BRILLIANT

Pick nice!

You can be both but numerous studies have repeatedly shown that a high IQ is no guarantee of success. In fact, it has been said that intelligence is like a 4-wheel drive vehicle—it'll take you farther off road before you get stuck! *Be the kind of person your dog thinks you are.*

The longest 3 years of my life....

5th grade!

I graduated in the upper 90th percentile of my class!

Of course, a low IQ doesn't help much but what is important is emotional intelligence. The book *Emotional Intelligence* by Daniel Goleman was published in 1995 and continues to be widely quoted. The qualities of an emotionally intelligent person are

Optimism	Empathetic, compassionate
Mature	Calm, in control of his emotions
Coping skills	Patient, tolerates delayed gratification
People skills	Social intelligence
Self discipline	Emotional savvy
Poised	Good self-esteem

Nothing listed here has to do with intelligence, genius or brilliance, but the people with the above characteristics tend to be the most successful and probably happier than most. Are we putting too much emphasis on MCAT scores for selection into medical school and not enough on assessing emotional intelligence?

♦ **The "C" students run the world!** (Harry S Truman)

Can we improve emotional intelligence in medical students and young physicians? I don't know for certain, but I think we can through role models and mentoring. Physicians lacking in social skills probably shouldn't be practicing medicine.

♦ **Did you ever notice how few great composers come out of the Ku Klux Klan?** (George Carlin)

♦ **A pessimist is an optimist that has the facts!**

Emotionally intelligent people are better able to handle their own emotions. Interestingly, people that suppress facial expressions in response to various emotions have heightened measurable physiologic responses such as pulse, skin conductance and temperature.

Inherent in possessing the qualities listed above is that the person is nice, nice to be around and nice to work with or for. Sure, there are many successful CEOs and managers and entrepreneurs who aren't nice but are they truly successful in the minds of the people around them? It depends on your definition of success. Are they respected? Can you recall the position they attained without also remembering they are also jerks? Physicians are (should be) people oriented and, in order to practice the art of medicine effectively, must be nice.

So hard to get along with,
A bunch of Quakers beat him up!

A man walks up to the clerk in a book store and asks
Where the self-help section is.
She says if she told him it would defeat its purpose!

THE MAYO CULTURE OF CARING

Shortly after I self-published the first edition of this book, one of the leaders of our Allied Health Personnel (AHP) read my book and asked me if I would give a talk to about 800 of our AHP from some thoughts she read in the book (she didn't tell me initially that it would be 18 talks over 5 days to 40+ people at a time in order to not disrupt the functioning of the work area they came from!) which I did gladly knowing that it would be a challenge and that I could learn and adjust my talk accordingly for the next group. However, I didn't want to stand in front of them and read sections out of my book! Instead, because I personally think our AHP are one of the absolute strengths of Mayo's longevity of around 100 years, I directed my talks to what I thought their role was and is in Mayo's success. Many of the AHP have had family working at the Clinic for decades, long before many of them were even born; they are part of the heritage.

Also, during my many years at the Clinic, I have been asked multiple times by patients and friends why the Clinic is so 'famous'?, "what is its secret?" Giving these talks allowed me to think out what I feel is its "secret" for being one of the best medical centers in the world. It fits in with one of the themes of my book—The Art of Medicine, realizing that to care about patients you don't have to be a physician.

In our process of Continuous Improvement, we always invoke the mantras of The Mayo Culture, The Mayo Clinic Model of Caring, and The Mayo Clinic Model of Care and its associated service elements. I put all these together into The Mayo Culture of Caring and it is what I attribute to why Mayo has been so successful for the last 100 years or so.

Mayo has several starting dates: In the summer of 1883 a disastrous tornado hit Rochester killing dozens of people. The Sisters of the Order of St Francis asked Dr William Worrell Mayo to move 100 miles to Rochester to develop a practice of medicine and if he would they would build him a hospital. In those days a hospital was a place you went to die, but they had other plans. He came and the 30 bed hospital was completed in 1889.

Other dates include 1883 when Dr. William (Will) Joseph Mayo finished medical school at the University of Michigan, and 1889 when Dr. Charles (Charlie) Horace Mayo completed medical school at Northwestern University in Chicago and joined their father in practice—The Mayo Clinic, and alternatively the "Mayo Brothers" clinic. Or, in 1901 when Dr Henry Plummer, an internist practicing 30 miles south of Rochester was hired. The word 'genius' is an overused word but not when it came to Henry Plummer. What he developed in the next decade is still used today—the uniform medical record, the exam table which has been copied and used around the world, a tube system for sending blood and tissue samples and medical records and x-rays around the clinic system, and much, much more.

And finally, 1914 when probably the first ever building in the world opened—The 1914 Building— dedicated to the integrated group practice of medicine. By then the Mayos were hiring many very competent physicians in different specialties, or creating the specialties that were unheard of up to this time.

With my nearly 50 years at Mayo, I can say that I have participated in, contributed to, witnessed, and benefited from Mayo's Culture of Caring. I relished any opportunity to explain my feelings of this culture that I feel is unique to anyone that will listen in the hopes that we will never lose this Art of Medicine, pointing out that for many reasons it is being de-emphasized and lost everywhere around the world. And given the opportunity to speak eventually to over 2000 allied health personnel, nurses and physicians at Mayo on the Mayo Culture of Caring allowed me to personally thank them for their tremendous contributions to Mayo.

There are a number of unique strengths to Mayo Clinic that have greatly contributed to its success:

1) The genius of Will and Charlie Mayo—the Mozarts of medicine, I call them. I can't ignore the contributions of the nuns of the Order of St Francis who, without any experience in building and running a hospital, were amazing. And, the genius of Henry Plummer. The Mayos described their practice of medicine as "...an experiment in cooperative individualism".

2) Physician leadership. The governance has always been physicians and always will be per the by-laws. We have an extensive committee system that all physicians are encouraged to participate in.

3) We are salaried, minimizing any temptation to order tests and do procedures unnecessarily.

Family Concept

4) There was never an attempt, at least in writing, that Mayo employees would be considered as family but it is my feeling that this is what evolved early on. At the turn of the century a town of 1000 was a megalopolis to young women coming off the farms, or very small towns to seek employment. Just as they bonded with their extended families, new neighbors, and church members, they did so with the new friends they met at their employment with Mayo. Everyone seems to care about each other. This is the difference between mediocrity and greatness, as Vince Lombardi pointed out. Our turn over rate was and is very low.

5) Role models. I have been blessed with outstanding role models from day one. Not just the 30 or so pulmonologists that I interacted with every day, but all the internists/subspecialists, many surgeons, pathologists, radiologists, pediatricians, etc. I knew them all and benefited greatly from their qualities. I also learned from the allied health personnel who were also my role models. Not only did I relate to superior quality but also quantity. I never really appreciated the full value of role models until after many years on the staff. They were all extended *family.*

6) Integrated group practice. This is teamwork. I could pick up the phone and talk to a world's authority about my patient. Or, they came to my office to see the patient in consultation and I could learn more about the disease and the patient. As many patients have said, somewhat in surprise, *The doctors actually talk to each other!*

7) Allied Health Personnel (AHP) plus the nurses and administrators. I would tell them that they, especially the allied health personnel and the administrators, that they are health care professionals (the nurses knew they were professionals), with a health care professional being someone with extra training in people skills with an obligation to society. And they would say they didn't have any formal training in

this and no plaque on the wall. I would then point out that they got their training at home. They brought with them a tremendous Scandinavian work ethic and "...didn't know the difference than to be nice to the patients and each other!" They didn't come from broken or dysfunctional families—you can't buy this kind of employee nor train them to be the way they are. Many of our employees, including some physicians, have had parents and grandparents who worked for the Clinic.

8) High quality, caring physicians and scientists. Prima donnas don't usually last very long at Mayo—they see that they don't fit in.

9) Finally, we live by the creed that **The Needs of the Patient Come First!**

NEVER underestimate the power of your caring!

These 'strengths' contribute to the Mayo Culture of Caring. But there is more to it than that. I previously mentioned the *Butterfly Effect*, where the nebulous but not disproven concept of a butterfly flapping her wings 1000 miles away can affect your local weather. At Mayo, a single act of caring is like a butterfly flapping its wings, producing a small increment of improvement in our patient's health and well being through the science of caring. Add to this dozens and dozens of acts of caring over the course of the patient's experience at Mayo and now we can begin to see its benefits.

Everyone was so nice at Mayo,
And,
Oh yes, they cured my cancer!

I've heard this story many times, starting off how nice everyone was and then adding that 'they cured my cancer', or found the cause of my pain, etc. And this isn't unique to Mayo by any means, but it points out the value the patient and family put on caring, the butterfly effect again. Another similar story: "Mayo is the most pleasant place I have visited. Everyone has been so nice. Even the patients are friendly!" Even the patients pick up on the butterfly effect and pass it on!

As I'll discuss in the next section, there is definite science in the act of caring. We now know why patients benefit scientifically from being surrounded by a caring atmosphere. It is thousands of Mayo employees including physicians flapping their wings of caring. Even if an employee doesn't interact with the patients, their caring for each other behind the scenes trickles up to the employees that do. It's a family thing.

But what is a culture? The dictionary doesn't describe our type of culture. My definition is that it is a positive cooperative environment that takes at least 2 or 3 generations to develop. It is a people thing. It amounts to your reputation, to the institution's reputation. It can't occur in a start up business or hospital. It is a sense of family working in unity as a team.

A positive culture engenders loyalty and pride and is shaped by the totality of each other's positive interactions. From this you can see that it might be considered a 'glue' that builds trust within the institution and contributes to individual and institutional vitality.

There aren't many successful companies with a negative culture. For those that exist, they are dysfunctional with high turnover rate and no sense of family. There are very few positive role models.

Pride is hard to describe but we know how we feel when our team, be it high school, college or professional, wins the 'big one'. You feel great for a few weeks; you have bragging rights for this period. I tell our employees that Mayo wins the Super Bowl, the World Series, the NCAA finals, the Masters and so on every day; we just don't have a parade the next day. But every day they should remind themselves on their way to work that they need to take great pride in the fact that they work for, and contribute to, one of the best medical institutions in the world. This pride makes you want to do your best as an integral part of the team. The bar is high. It brings the *family* of Mayo people closer together. As I've said previously, I think one of the secrets of Mayo's success is the feeling of family—we care about each other, and the professional progress of each and every member.

♦ **Pride is the quality that separates excellence from mediocrity!**

**We cannot all be great, but we can always attach
Ourselves to something that is great! This
Is the Pride of working for a great institution!**

As a result of being a member of the Mayo Family, we need to remind ourselves also that the patients are our guests, that we are their hosts, and to treat them accordingly. I think we do that because of the strong family concepts at home that they bring to work with them.

Every patient is the only patient!

But we can't rest on our laurels.

**The future of the Mayo Clinic depends on
The Quality of the care given!**
Len Berry

**People don't buy a Cadillac because
They think GM needs the money!**

The patients come to us for one reason and one only, to get an answer to their health concerns. We have practiced *continuous improvement* here long before it was in vogue. We have always been looking toward the best way to diagnose and treat our patients, i.e., stay at the cutting edge. If we don't provide the best care including the art as well as the science of medicine, we won't continue for the next 100 years. We should aim to be world's authorities in caring!

I like to point out the similarity of an iceberg and the practice of medicine here. From science class we learned that 90% of an iceberg resides below the water level. It takes about 9 allied health personnel to support one practicing clinician, the portion of the iceberg above the water. If one or two of the 9 become counterproductive through a negative attitude, uncooperativeness, bring anger from home to work, the iceberg will be in trouble, resulting in less efficient production by the clinician. Remember the story I gave about the 2 stone cutters? What kind of stone cutter are you? Just showing up for work, or building a beautiful cathedral?

At this point I show the audience my Circle of Happiness and point out the value, not just at work at Mayo but at home, church, everywhere, of completing this circle. As a result, one other strength we have is that the vast majority of our employees from the very beginning work with a good attitude and do complete the circle with a significant amount of happiness. Our patients recognize this. The role models and family concept contribute to this.

When you are working in a family environment as I think we are, you are more likely to follow the Platinum Rule of Medicine, which as I've stated earlier is to treat each patient like you would want a member of your family treated. You can never go wrong with this goal.

At the end of my presentation to the allied health personnel, nurses, administrators and physicians, I make a point of thanking them for their significant contribution to Mayo's Culture of Caring!

We know it works in practice, but
Do we know it will work in theory?

The Mayo brothers made the integrated practice of medicine work before anyone theorized about it! They just did it.

THE SCIENCE OF CARING

As of the last few decades this has become a brand new discipline. Some might see this topic as a description of how a psychologist brings about a change in someone's psyche through dialogue, as it is on a multitude of hits on a google search, but I refer to it as a hard science of chemicals we can measure in the blood and changes that can be seen on the brain PET scan and functional brain MRI. I've briefly mentioned these when I wrote about happiness, attitude and kindness.

This discussion on the science of caring will be out of date quickly as this science is advancing rapidly. No doubt pharmaceutical companies would love to isolate, mass produce and then sell a hormone that produces kindness and happiness, and maybe even marital bliss, such that I'm certain that they are working on this now.

However, I'm going to list and discuss what I know as this data tends to confirm that kindness and caring are chemically, physiologically, antiinflammatorily, neuropharmacologically, neuroendocinologically and immunologically capable of improving well-being while at the same time healing. And the reason I mention this is that it is easier for a patient to know that the reason they feel so depressed or miserable and unhappy is that chemical and neurophysiological changes are occurring and that it "isn't all in my head", even though it is.

The following table lists just some of the substances that have been found to be increased or decreased with the proposed resultant effects. It is also known that nervous tissue pathways can affect the receptor surface of many different immune cells, ultimately affecting the immunocompetency of the host.

Increased	Result/associated with
Phenthylamine	Elation
Dopamine	Energized
Endorphins	Runner's high; other positive
Oxytocin (hugging, holding, the 'cuddle' hormone)	Bonding, feeling of connection, attachment, trust
Prolactin	Nurturing
Immunoglobulins	Healing; anti-infection
Vasopressin	Recognizing someone as familiar
Neuro growth factors from exercise	Reduces risk of dementia
C-Reactive protein (CRP)	Inflammation

STRESS

Anesthesiologist's reassuring words as patient goes to sleep	Less post op complications, shorter hospital stay
↓Cytokines	Slower wound healing
↑Cortisols	↑BP, slower healing, depression

85

↑Fibrinogen	↑blood viscosity and platelet aggregation leading to intravascular thrombosis/stroke and heart attack
↑Epinephrine and norepinephrine	↑BP, tachycardia, vasoconstriction
Noise	↑Cortisols, epinephrine, norepinephrine
T lymphocyte impairment	↓Vaccination response
Forgiveness	↓BP and pulse rate

This is an incomplete list but gives some idea of the complexity of the human mind. Also most of these chemicals are eventually broken down in the body to metabolites that we don't always know much about but can be an even greater mediator of end results than their predecessors.

I can't help but wonder how much disease we bring on ourselves with stress. I didn't list the studies showing that stress can bring out latent viruses from our system to produce very serious diseases in those with an impaired immune system, or just the common cold in any of us. Add sleep deprivation to the stress and you can see why some people seem to be sick all the time. But we don't know much about what sleep does, or lack of sleep causes in the way of psychobiology.

Pet therapy is a real thing; there are a lot of scientific but mostly anecdotal studies showing that being able to touch a pet can reduce high blood pressure, rapid breathing and muscle tension. There are reports of patients waking up from a coma seemingly just from putting the patient's hand on a dog's head. Raised levels of endorphins and lowered levels of cortisols and epinephrine (adrenalin) have been measured in response to pet therapy, and it isn't just from touching and petting a pet. Their very presence seems to have this measurable effect. The author of this study said that, "A chronic state of arousal isn't healthy; it causes hypertension, and it has been implicated in diabetes, asthma, and various gastrointestinal disorders. Part of the arousal response is to turn off the immune system, so you are breaking down instead of healing yourself." In the same study the blood pressure dropped 10% in those patients visited by a dog, whereas it went up in a number who had a human visitor! Stress!!!

It has been found that patients with physical disabilities that just by walking with a trained dog alongside allows them to walk more confidently and as a result, walk farther and faster. Pet owners are more likely to survive a heart attack, keeping in mind that the pet(s) doesn't rejoin their owner until they get home from the hospital. Maybe it is the thought and desire to return home to their pet that wills the patient to get better. Endorphins again? The unleashed power of the mind!

There is a study reported in the medical literature of the beneficial effects of the relief of mild depression after spending time every day with dolphins including petting them. Their response was compared to same number of patients (controls) who also spent time at same beach resort but had no access to the dolphins, whose depression scores did not improve.

We have no idea of what touching pets and dolphins does to the psychobiology, but there are too many positive reports testifying to the benefits to write them off as quirky. Children with affective and other disorders are particularly benefited with having a pet at home. Seniors with pets, even tropical fish, have less physician contact visits than those without. Their blood pressure is lower, their lipids are better, and they have better psychological well-being, possibly because of less loneliness. Pets in nursing homes increase the verbal and social interactions. Need I say more on behalf of pets?

I have previously mentioned the findings on the PET scans and brain functional MRIs. This kind of research will only increase. Now, there is some therapeutic benefit to the use of functional MRIs: Patients with chronic pain such as fibromyalgia using 'real-time' MRI, meaning they themselves could view the rostral anterior cingulated cortex (one of the brain's pain centers) on their own MRI while they are having the procedure done, and somehow over several 13 minute sessions manipulate and suppress the activity in this center with over 50% reduction in the pain! The patients themselves could not explain what they were doing to do this but it was effective in 5 of the 8 in the study.

I'll say it again, the mind (whatever that is) is obviously very powerful. The physician and the public (the patient) cannot ignore this power in order to maximize their health and well-being but they need to be taught how to do this, maybe beginning in grade school. This also explains why placebos often give the same beneficial effects that the blinded drug does in experimental trials.

I discuss stress later on but it is evident from all my reading that it accounts for a huge cost to productivity in the work place as well as a multitude of medical and psychiatric ills. Industry and the health care system can't afford this. A study reported in a psychiatry journal late 2005 and made the national news and many newspapers on stress in marriages. The authors created a blister on the skin of the arm with a vacuum pump, then, couples were asked to discuss various scenarios about their marriages. The blisters healed at only a 60% rate in the couples with considerable hostility compared to those with low hostility. The authors were able to correlate cytokine and other inflammatory peptides in the blood with the level of hostility and blister size.

I am repeating myself on the role of deep breathing but will do so again because more study needs to be done on this. To remind you, when the lungs are stretched to near maximum, impulses are sent to the brain stem as a message to stop inhaling as the lungs can't go any larger (the Hering-Breuer reflex). This same impulse must go on to other centers in the brain that has control over stress, as it has been shown that slow deep breaths can be very effective in reducing stress for the moment when done properly. And by this I mean sitting quietly, not doing anything else, and just thinking positive thoughts. The pharmaceutical industry won't like this—they can't sell you anything to make you deep breathe.

As I have already and will again, discuss the tremendous impact depression has on the individual and society. It is one of the more chronically debilitating illnesses there is in the world. It is the antithesis of happiness. We know that patients in congestive heart failure, also one of the most common chronic debilitating illnesses in this country, and with depression, do not live nearly as long as those without depression. Two chemicals probably play a major role in this: epinephrine and fibrinogen. With propensity to form clots in the small coronary arteries from an elevated fibrinogen, the results are obvious—gradually diminished blood flow to the already diseased myocardium.

Two-thirds of the patients with major depression suffered early life trauma. Their brains became hard-wired way back then. But in many this has been suppressed without ever being able to deal with it as an adult. This has begettened heightened negativity along with an increase in hyperphysiologic endocrine stimulation of various organs in the body and in turn physical symptoms.

I'm beginning to think that teaching children in grade school and thereafter how to meditate and do yoga and encourage them to do it every day for the rest of their lives could ultimately save trillions of dollars in many ways! Many businesses, including some with tens of thousands of employees are doing just this. Work places need to have set aside locations where the employee can retreat to (quiet meditation rooms or cubicles) in order to do this during the day, in addition to doing it at home. And more scientific study needs to be done over a long period of time to assess why this works and how. Just setting aside 10 to 15 minutes one to three times a day in a quiet place to deep breathe may be all that is necessary for some people after they've learned the value of mindfulness and meditation. In fact, maybe just 2 or 3 minute breaks might be all that is needed at a time for some that have experience with meditation.

We do know a good bit about the effects of meditation on the brain. As mentioned in the discussion on happiness, the left pre-frontal cortex of the brain highlights with happiness. I don't think we know much about the chemical changes except there is an increase in some endorphins and decrease in cortisol. A more recent study found that daily meditation thickens the gray matter of the brain, the working part of the cortex, in areas of mindfulness, memory, decision making as well as the happiness area. And it may slow the naturally occurring thinning in the area of the cortex that occurs with age. And these patients have more energy, comparable to that of a good night's sleep in the non meditators.

Post traumatic stress syndrome (PTSD) is real, it can be seen on brain imaging studies. With psychotherapy (so far, not with medication except maybe with beta blockers rather than psychotropic drugs), it is reversible in many. But not many who have been severely stressed in childhood can afford psychotherapy. Beta blockers, and only those beta blockers than get through the blood-brain barrier, block the receptors to epinephrine (adrenalin) and norepinephrine. A lot of work is being done along these lines.

Our friend cortisol, seems to be lower in the brains of some people with PTSD from acute medical illnesses and giving low doses of the hormone reduces the symptoms of the stress, while giving another chemical, glutamate, seems to enhance the normal memory extinction process when administered right after the traumatic event.

Noise. We take for granted that we have to live with the pervasive noise that is everywhere. Some experts have described a new disease: Vibroacoustic disease that is any number of symptoms as a result of exposure to chronic noise in the 50 plus decibel range, and especially when over 80 decibels. Many hyped up car stereos and now MP3 players are well over 100 decibels, and some over 130! Street traffic is around 80 decibels. This leads to a heightened stress response due to elevated cortisols and epinephrine, the long term results being hypertension and faster resting pulse rate. I don't know of any (yet) head MRI or PET scan studies related to long term high noise exposure, but I suspect they will be abnormal. The question will be, how reversible are the changes? Our youth may be in for even more trouble from stress as a result of rock concerts, MP3 turned up to the max, and so on.

Where do genes come in to play a role? Or more importantly, the expression of genes on the psyche? We know a lot about genes and diseases but little about genes in our response to stress. Proteomics is the study of proteins (amino acids) expressed by genes and as of now there isn't much information available, but there will be. These proteins likely play a huge role that we will be learning more about in time.

Note that I haven't mentioned anything about studies of what is occurring in the blood or brain of angry and hateful people but this will come, on the hope that scientists will come up with ways of reversing these changes. I am a believer that there may be a hate gene that is present in about 5 to 10% of the population. In most people the only effect it has is producing angry, unhappy people with limited social skills, misfits. All have low emotional intelligence. But, when confronted with unbearable stresses, usually beginning in childhood, possibly provoked by what they see on television, begin acting out with violence and hate crimes. Most are loners and then for the first time in their life find people with similar anger and hate who accept them because of this. And, if a group of them get organized, with the militia and anti-Western terrorists being good examples, anything is possible. All have a common theme—their repulsion against authority. Identifying these people at birth and being able to do something about it (George Orwell-like) could save a lot of grief.

What I have mentioned here will likely create a new kind of therapist, someone who will treat patients with either normally occurring but diminished levels of hormones, endorphins and peptides in the blood, or with drugs that will block the effects of these normally present chemicals but in elevated amounts. We are talking about probably a billion or more people who could benefit from this kind of therapy! At a dollar a pill a day, do the math. I will call this person a psychobiologist, who will have training in psychology, neuro and endocrine pharmacology and biology. I see a great future in this area.

Wherever the art of medicine is loved,
There is also love of humanity!
                              Hippocrates

A good relationship between the patient and the physician
Is something of a victory in itself.
That victory is made possible because the physician
Attaches as much importance to the patient's
Psychobiologic needs as he does to the patient's
Physiologic needs!
                              Sir William Osler

One meets with many men who stood high in their classes,
Who have great knowledge of medicine but,
Very little wisdom in application. They have
Mastered the science but have failed in
The understanding of the human being!
                              WJ Mayo

Healing behaviors that relieve suffering are as
Important as knowledge and skills!

A moment of peace and personal empathy will do more than
Hours of academic instruction!
                              Sebastian Fetscher

These quotes on the Art of Medicine are self-explanatory. The human mind is almost unfathomable. I doubt that artificial intelligence will ever comprehend or duplicate the mind! Knowing that emotions and so many of the bodily functions are controlled by the mind and that unless the physician deals with these, the outcome including the patient's satisfaction will be far less than anticipated and hoped for. Our profession isn't a doctor dealing with a disease, it is a human being coming to you with a problem. *Machines can help decide but only physicians can heal!*

♦ **A doctor doesn't choose his patients; instead, he has been chosen**
   to receive a gift of trust!

Care more particularly for the individual
Patient than the special features of the disease!
                              Sir William Osler

Another infrequently used term in the medical literature is the *Art of Caring,* but anyone can practice the art of caring—only the physician can practice the Art of Medicine. *Treading on the patient's soul engenders trust!*

The Art of Medicine consists of amusing the patient
While nature cures the disease!
                              Voltaire

The Art of Medicine can be learned,
But it can't be taught!

I don't believe you can teach the Art of Living or the Art of Medicine; you can't tell a medical student to be nice to that patient and expect it to always happen, but you can guide them through some do's and don'ts. When the student or resident gets in a room with the patient and their family, it is somewhat out of your control, but at least until you can get some feedback from the patient or you can personally observe the interactions and then discuss it with the young physician. The same with your children. You can't force them to be nice, to be happy, to enjoy life—they have to learn it from you, by observing you and not from what you tell them—*actions speak louder than words.*

The essence of development of the caring person, someone with significant emotional intelligence, begins at birth and is strongly fortified by age 3 to 5 years. Thereafter, it is nurtured (hopefully) by the family, society and other role models. Unfortunately, we are in a crisis for good role models in all walks of life. By the time the future physician is in medical school, this part of their development is far behind them.

The only other way of 'teaching' the art of medicine is through role models and mentoring. *I think role models are the absolute key in allowing the young physician to 'learn' the art of medicine, assuming there is some feedback to the learner and nurturing of already inherent people skills by mentors.* Success in life for anyone requires role models and mentoring. Where does it say that young people have the wisdom and experience to be on their own? The adage, "They have to learn it the hard way just like I did" is unfair and arrogant.

By virtue of our attainment in life as physicians, we are already looked up to as role models whether we like it or not. You become the energy and the strength of the people around you, including your patients and paramedical support personnel. Of course, a negative energy creates stress! We have allowed ourselves to be put on a pedestal, and unfortunately, for many this has fostered arrogance.

I know I'm looked up to as a
Role model and
I take this very seriously!
Mia Hamm
US Ladies Soccer Team Star

Just as Mia Hamm does we physicians, parents, leaders, and others must take this obligation seriously. *And we must become what we wish to teach!* The young physicians can't learn the art of medicine out of a book. We must do all we can to restore the public's trust in us by acting like the kind of physician we should be and serving as a role model to others. *Would you want to be cared for by a physician like yourself?*

We are in need of a better more professionally
Uplifting bond than money
To hold the profession together!
Paul Elwood

We must continuously ask ourselves how we can improve our own qualities which are being observed by all those around us, not just other physicians but other health personnel, our patients and especially by our families. *This becomes an action of personal continuous improvement.* The goals you set should be the change you want to see in the world. How we act relates to our own level of self-esteem.

- **♦ If you know you are a role model, how do you want to be remembered?**

We become what we wish to 'teach', i.e., what we want others to learn from us. All mentors are, or should be, positive role models but not all ideal role models are mentors. I call the latter 'silent mentoring'. Most mentors are senior to their mentees while role models can be any age. I have learned a tremendous amount of the art of medicine from physicians much younger than me as well as from paramedical health personnel. But you must be willing to learn and to change, no matter how old you are.

I recall visiting a patient on my service in the hospital some years ago. With me that day were 3 internal medicine residents, a pulmonary trainee and a medical student (too many but patients seemed to accept this). The young resident whose patient this was got a page as we entered the room. He returned shortly while we were talking to the patient. He worked his way through the crowd in the hospital room and without interrupting anything, took the patient's hand. A warm glow came over her face, probably accomplishing more than all the medications we were giving her! We all learned from this resident.

As we grow older one of the most rewarding things we can do is mentor young physicians. The true professional sees this as a responsibility. This is a way of passing on what you think is important, your virtues, your values, your own professionalism; these will always be remembered by your mentees.

- **♦ Every man I meet is my superior in some way in that I can learn from him!** (Ralph Waldo Emerson)

- **♦ I can always be certain of learning from those I am with. There will be good qualities that I can select for imitation and bad ones that will teach me what requires correction in myself!** (Confucius)

Not everyone is like Confucius in that they are not willing to learn from others—their ego is too great (arrogance), their self-esteem is too low, they lack humility, or maybe they are depressed or angry. How often do we see physicians failing to practice the art of medicine in spite of the presence of excellent role model physicians around them that they could learn from. No matter what age we are we need to look to the people around us and draw on their positive attributes, making a mental note, and later a written note, of how we can improve ourselves (see section on Write-Therapy). Many physicians, unfortunately, feel that because they are at the cutting edge of technology, and that they are delivering this to the patient, they don't have to practice the Art of Medicine, and the patient should be grateful for this!

I'm certain the good traits you like in others, you already have, you just need to further develop and use them. *You are never too old to have role models, as you will not live long enough to learn from all the mistakes by yourself!*

**Trying to do the best for your patients
Must be the major motivating force in your effort
To remain competent!**
Dwight C. McGoon

Dwight McGoon, along with my father who was an internist and probably forgot more medicine than I knew, was one of my greatest role models. He was a cardiac surgeon that I interacted with on occasion as a pulmonologist; even though I was young and new on the staff, he knew who I was. He didn't pat me on the back or tell me I was doing a great job. He didn't have to. He exuded a warmth and a caring in his smile and his demeanor. He practiced the Art of Medicine and the Art of Living without even having to say a word. Besides this he was a terrific surgeon. His patients loved him.

   ♦ **The doctor is a powerful placebo!**

**You have made us a little bit better
Because we have known you!**

COMMUNICATION

I was misquoted in my autobiography!
Charles Barkley
NBA star

Effective communication is one of the most important skills anyone can have and is probably the most important aspect in practicing the Art of Medicine. Volumes have been written on communication skills dealing with all aspects of life, not just the patient-physician encounter. In the medical world lack of (or ineffective/misunderstood/misinterpreted) communication is the single most common cause of instigation of malpractice lawsuits. It is also the top complaint patients have about their physician and one of the most common reasons they change physicians or seek alternative/complementary medicine. Properly done, it has been shown in surgical patients on the part of the surgeon and the anesthesiologist to significantly shorten a hospital stay, reduce complications, and accelerate recovery. It is strongly related to patient satisfaction. It is powerful, including the negative as well as the positive. But communication is much, much more than the exchange of words.

There are 2 styles of communication: 1) authoritative, domineering, professionally detached, or 2) affiliative, empathetic, non judgmental, interested. Which one are you? The best place to teach communication to your children is around the dinner table.

♦ **Seek first to understand, then to be understood!** (Stephen Covey)

I never thought anything about **body language** until I read that communication experts say that 90% of personal person-to-person communication is nonverbal! I would have guessed that it would be closer to 15 to 20%. This being the case, then body language and listening as a form of communication become ever so important in the patient-physician interaction. There are very few formalized relationships in which so much critical information can be exchanged without saying anything as there is between the patient and the physician.

Body language helps explain the chemistry that can occur between 2 people, even though we don't fully understand it. Some believe in the 'aura' phenomenon. Fish produce electromagnetic energy; most insects and animals secrete pheromones. How do we explain a trained dog's ability to detect and warn its master of an impending seizure minutes before it occurs? Through specialized and elaborate photography, it has been possible to photograph 'aura' around plants and flowers. What do we emanate?

♦ **It's amazing how much you'll hear when no one is talking!**

In 1970 Jules Fast published his book entitled *Body Language.* Its release made the national news. On the book jacket was an attractive woman sitting on a chair; I assumed that it was mostly about being seductive and never read it, until now. It is far more than the role of seduction.

He points out mannerisms, facial expressions (the face can register over 7000 different expressions, mostly micro-expressions), body movements, that for the most part are unintentional and automatic and not thought of as a way of communicating on a moment to moment basis. But if communication is mostly nonverbal then body language says a lot!

♦ **The best way to improve your body language is to improve your attitude!**

As individuals we don't appreciate what messages we send with our bodies, and most of the time we have no comprehension of how they are received. Some people are much more adept and skilled in reading and interpreting other people, including many of our patients. They can intuitively and quickly size up if the physician is truly interested in them before he or she even says anything. And many can and will do this within the first 5 seconds of seeing the physician.

Studies have shown that patient satisfaction significantly correlates with the physician's nonverbal communicating skills, especially if the physician was adept at genuinely expressing emotions non verbally and receiving and acting on nonverbal emotional cues from the patient. This is empathy. And this becomes all the more important if the patient is unable to verbally express emotions, at least until trust is established.

To the computer-camera, our face may be as unique as fingerprints, voice, retina or iris. So much can be portrayed, both good and bad, by our facial expression. Work at the Salk Institute with the Facial Action Coding System (FACS) has shown that micro expressions of the face lasting only 0.1 second can be read and interpreted by the computer slow motion camera. Some people can do this subconsciously and make very accurate intuitive judgments about that person. The more a person talks the more facial expressions they make, so if you are trying to interpret a persons emotions, keep them talking!

The FACS group has certified over 500 people to read facial expressions with uncanny accuracy. Jury consultants study facial expressions during a juror's interview to decide what kind of person they are. NASA has a multi million dollar contract to study astronaut's facial expressions on long journeys to places like Mars, if and when they occur. They are concerned with severe depression or even murder due to the unpredictable degrees of stress of these flights lasting years.

In 2004 a study was done where 70% of the winners of the US Senate race were accurately predicted on facial appearances where the interpreters didn't know anything about the 2 candidates whose facial pictures they judged from. Competence rather than a baby face was the deciding factor.

The face as well as the voice can register 6 different easily recognizable emotions which are happiness, fear, anger, sadness, surprise and disgust. How many last only 0.1 second? How much control do we have over our facial expressions and tone of voice? Do our emotions override the face we try to put on? I suspect so.

Body posture can sometimes express fear more than the face.

Considerable nonverbal communication is through the eyes. Appropriate eye contact is imperative; it should be passive, rather than staring down or intimidating the receiver, while still conveying a sense of caring. *The eyes are the pathway to the soul.* When dealing with difficult situations, maintaining eye contact can soften the atmosphere and portray a sense of listening, which you should be doing anyway. It helps accelerate the mutual bonding necessary to establish trust, while at the same time sharing the control between the 2 people involved. I am impressed how some people have mastered the ability to avoid eye contact. This is one sign of low self-esteem.

A Smile:
The shortest distance between 2 people!

A smile is an expression of warmth, of caring and is one of the strongest positive nonverbal means of communicating. It is truly universal language of kindness, and it costs nothing. It's a day softener. That's why I have it in my Circle of Happiness. The memory of it can last hours. It takes 72 muscles to frown and only 14 to smile, and there is more information in a smile. It has been estimated that there are as many as 20 different kinds of smiles! Smiling not only releases endorphins in you but also in the person(s) receiving it. It also appears to enhance your immune system. A smile should be spontaneous and genuine, as a forced smile is insincere and obvious to the receiver. Try thinking a good thought, or do a small act of kindness—a genuine smile will come easier. (A false smile does not involve the muscles around the eyes). However, a smile isn't mostly the mouth shape. The next time you look at a picture of the Mona Lisa, block off the mouth and note that you can see a beautiful smile in her eyes.

Smiling is infectious, you catch it like the flu.
When someone smiled at me today,
I started smiling too.
I passed around the corner and someone saw my grin.
When he smiled I realized that I had passed it on to him.
I thought about that smile, then I realized its worth.
A single smile, just like mine, could travel round the earth!

A smile can disarm an angry patient. It has a calming effect and can be infectious. It implies that you are in control of yourself. It says 'welcome to the moment'. It can even be appropriate to the terminally ill or very sick patient, providing it is given in the context of affording hope. *You can't have a genuine smile without compassion.* And the more you smile the more compassion you will have. You can usually make a crying child stop crying by getting them to force a smile.

Interestingly, a study was done of a 30 year follow-up of women where those who were smiling in their college year-book picture were happier, went through fewer divorces and were more accomplished than those who weren't smiling!

♦ **I've never seen anyone that was smiling that wasn't beautiful!**

A frown rarely accomplishes anything good and may be greatly misinterpreted; the patient may think you are not telling them everything. The same goes for low-grade mumbles and "hmmmm", or "Uh oh". The only time a frown is appropriate is when silently empathizing with a patient as he or she describes their pains and sorrows.

Look relaxed, even if you are behind in your schedule. Sit down. The patient will then overestimate the time you spent with them. Put your pen down. Lean back in your chair and listen. Caution on drumming the desk top or twiddling your pen—your patient may interpret this as impatience or boredom on your part. Ideally you should be at eye level with the patient, and if you are dealing with a difficult patient, then maybe even a few inches below their eye level. This gives them some sense of control. To show concern, if necessary, on a few occasions, lean forward towards the patient for a few moments. But respect their sacred space. There are times when it is important to not have your desk between you and the patient.

At the bedside I like to sit down beside the patient so they can easily see me rather than stand at the bedside or foot of the bed, assuming some discussion is needed about their illness. In spite of the controversy over this, I personally have no problem sitting on the side of the bed, with a few exceptions.

Even if the patient is on a ventilator, try to communicate with them the best way possible. Takes more time but they need you. Even the comatose or sedated patient probably benefits from you talking to them by their name and squeezing their arm or hand. Personally adjust their pillow, put a cool cloth on their forehead. It gives you, the physician, a sense of bonding to the patient. Offer them some hope. If you are their regular physician, they'll know your voice. It is said that in the semi-comatose or dying patient, hearing is the last sense to go. That is why words and the tone in which they are used are so important, even though they make up only 10% of communication.

Our **voice** probably gives us away much more than we know. It can express the 6 emotions mentioned and to a wide range. Many of us can't hide in our voice our true feelings about the person we are interacting with, to the point of giving them negative feedback.

Some feel that voice analysis is more sensitive than a lie detector test. Just like when we know our children aren't telling the truth. Probably many people (our patients) have an ability to micro analyze our voice and judge the sincerity of the message.

There is a device which filters out the verbal part of the voice leaving only the tone in which something is said. It's possible the patient blocks out the words and hears only the tone we're speaking in; in fact, I'm certain of this as over the years I've talked to a number of patients who don't seem to hear what I'm saying, yet they are engaged— they unconsciously may be trying to interpret the tone of my voice! Is the tone of your voice condescending, even if your words aren't?

It's been shown that some people, including physicians, can't truly express in the proper tone they wish to use to express an emotion, and it comes out the opposite way, usually negative instead of positive! This is why actors study elocution. They also study body language and now police are being taught this to help them when encountering suspects in crime—their careers depend on it! Don't ours! If the physician is angry about something, or depressed, or chronically ill, or just stressed, can he hide this from his voice, his body language? No! This is especially true of your attitude.

In dealing with patients who don't understand the language you are speaking, the only thing the person can go on is your body language, your facial expression, the inflection of your voice. They watch you while listening to the interpreter. And what are you doing while the interpreter is speaking to the patient? Looking bored?

Over 30 million citizens in this country don't speak English at home. Many of these know some English but certainly aren't conversant with medical terminology. Usually these patients won't tell the family member that is translating, sensitive medical information. And the family member who is translating, because of cultural mores, won't tell the patient he or she has cancer or another serious disease.

When dealing with a non English speaking patient, ideally a non family member acts as the interpreter. Look at the patient rather than the interpreter. Use multilingual patient education material. And when dealing with end of life issues, be sure you abide by their cultural rules, not yours. Some physicians and nurses overestimate their language skills when speaking a second language.

A careless word may kindle strife
A cruel word may wreck a life
A timely word may level stress
A loving word may heal and bless

I suppose we shouldn't have to measure our words but when the authoritative physician speaks to the vulnerable patient who hangs on every word, then we should think out what we are going to say, or not say(!) to the patient. Remember, *it's not what's said, it's what's heard!* Too often we say things before we even think of them!

♦ **Many people think with their mouth open!**

A few poor choice words can take away all hope. You can't retrieve these words, or 'strike them from the record.' As mentioned above many people, both patients and physicians, have difficulty expressing the emotions 'from which they speak,' and these may come out the opposite of what's desired. It is almost always the negative perception when the attempt is meant to be positive. Why isn't it the reverse? Maybe it is because 5 of the 6 emotions (fear, anger, sadness, surprise and disgust) are negatives (surprise can express happiness).

If the patient perceives he or she is getting good scientific care, then they aren't as concerned with the physician's body language, verbal and otherwise, but they won't have established as great a bonding and trust necessary for future care.

♦ **He couldn't lead a group in silent prayer!**

The placebo effect of words is powerful medicine. If the physician tells the patient to "...try this medicine, but I don't think it'll work", versus, "I think this medicine will really help you (while looking them in the eye), as many of my patients have seemed to have benefited from it for similar symptoms," can make a world of difference in the outcome.

An anesthesiologist's whispering reassuring words in the ear of the asleep patient has been found to lessen the post operative complications and shorten the hospital stay. The opposite is probably true in dealing with patients in the intensive care unit that is sedated or 'unresponsive' when we talk among ourselves at the bedside using negative words like, "I don't think he is going to make it," or "Uh oh, her blood pressure is dropping," or, "This looks bad," and so on. What does this do to the patient's subconscious mind? His endorphin production? It certainly must be the opposite of the calming words the anesthesiologist whispers in the patient's ear! The message and the way it is given by the physician regarding medication or therapy instructions is extremely important. Do you think the practitioner of alternative/complementary medicine speaks in negative tones? No way. That is part of their open secret. Through their words, and the effective physician's words, they will their desire to help the patient. And the patient is receptive to this.

The physician needs to show some control through his voice, in the process of making decisions of what to do next. When he or she says to the patient, *Tell me about it* (4 very powerful empathetic words), he needs to have a positive inflection in his voice. A wishy-washy indecisiveness makes the patient lose trust.

♦ He goes around the country stirring up apathy!

When assessing the patient, you need to constantly be mindful of what he or she is trying to tell you. By putting words in their mouth, like, "I think you're really worried about this aren't you?" or, "This has made you sad and depressed and helpless, hasn't it?," it short circuits to them that you are beginning to understand their real concerns and are more likely to open up right away. Consider ending up your conversation by saying, "Let me see if I understand what you're saying," and then summarize for them.

This kind of dialogue may be difficult in an academic center where the patient is reluctant to open up before the 'team' of 4 or 5 people. If the responsible, 'experienced' attending senses this, he or she should return alone or with only one housestaff and talk more about it. The patient may also be reluctant to open up in front of a member of the family in the room.

You can't be judgmental or overbearing or punitive, but you must maintain empathy in your words and your body language. Merely putting on a facial expression of empathy lights up a specific area of the brain on a functional MRI and leads to facilitating further empathy within yourself. Giving instructions or offering various alternatives on what step to take next always requires eye contact. The patient may then be better able to see what you're saying rather than hearing it!

In the physician-to-the-patient dialogue there can be several word messages but there is one class of words that I detest—I call them *cringe words.* Over the years patients many, many times have told me things other physicians or health care workers said to them. After a few words are out of their mouth, I can tell by the tone of their voice that I'm not going to like what I hear and I begin to cringe before they complete a sentence. These words are very hurtful to the patient and are a defamation to the profession of medicine. I always apologize to the patient, but I'm not sure why; I guess because I am embarrassed for my profession.

Dr Bernard Lown in his book *The Lost Art of Healing* says he has collected over 100 of these comments. I wish I had written down all the ones that I have heard as I've heard some real doozies, and certainly more than a 100 also. Remember, it's not what's said, it's what's heard; however, I have no doubt that what the patient related to me was probably pretty accurate. There are both sides to a story but it is the patient's perception that counts.

It is really incomprehensible to me that anyone, let alone a physician, could say these things to anyone, especially a person as vulnerable as a patient with real concerns. You can believe that these patients will tell many others what Dr X said, and maybe put it on the Internet! You'll never go wrong if you follow the old adage your mother taught you:

If you don't have anything nice to say,
Don't say anything!

You can't go wrong with this. In the business of medicine the patient is your customer. Once you start saying stupid, angry things, each time it gets easier and more automatic. In dealing with the vulnerable patient, and especially the difficult patient (more on this later), you must *think* (here is that 'thinking' again) about what you are going to say and use carefully chosen words. If you don't, it could come back to haunt you. Your patients hang on your every word, even if you think they don't.

The same goes for health care workers, especially nurses. The nurse may feel her comments are 'off the cuff' and unofficial, but for many hospitalized patients, they transfer their trust from the physician(s) to the nurses. I know of nurses telling the patient that a mistake was made in their care, more or less as a matter of social chatter! This may be the first the patient knows of it. If the nurse made the mistake such as giving the wrong medication, appropriate measures must be taken right away and noted in the record. The physician should be notified. If the physician made the mistake, it is his or her responsibility to tell the patient. The nurse needs to tell the physician what she told the patient.

If you don't know what you are talking about, keep quiet. I recall a very sick patient with end stage lung disease and an acute pneumothorax (collapsed lung) requiring a chest tube hooked up to a suction machine to re-expand his lung. The unit in the hospital where this would normally be managed was full, so he was put in another unit. A nurse came in and said, "I'll be your nurse for the next 12 hours." Then pointing to the suction machine attached to his chest tube said, "Oh, what's that?"

♦ **Talk is cheap because the supply exceeds the demand!**

In the following I'm going to give a number of examples of comments patients have told me over the years, or personal experiences of patients, or physicians who have been patients, that have been published in leading medical journals. Maybe it will make me feel better to share these so that some physicians will see themselves and hopefully amend their ways. The compassionate physician reading these will almost certainly cringe as I have and do.

> *It's your fault you're not getting any better.*
> *I don't think you want to get well.*
> *If you weren't so fat, you wouldn't have this problem.*
> *It's not important what you think.*
> *I'll do all the talking.*
> *I'm as good as they come—you don't need a second opinion.*
> *I need to dismiss you (from the ICU or the hospital)—we need the bed for someone we can help.*
> *You have one foot in the grave.*
> *He doesn't know what he is talking about; he's not a very good doctor. I wouldn't go back to him. Besides, he missed the diagnosis.*
> *You should have come to me sooner—I could have helped you then.*
> *There is nothing more to do; you might as well go home to die.*
> *First of all, get the idea of any chance of a cure out of your mind.*

♦ **His brain never had a thought his mouth couldn't use!**

> *I have absolutely nothing good to tell you about your tests—you're going to die.*
> *There's nothing wrong with you—it's all in your head.*
> *If you're a doctor, you can prescribe the medicine! If not, then shut up and let me be the doctor.*
> *That's the dumbest idea I ever heard (patient's idea).*
> *This could be a cancer. Why don't we wait a few months and see what happens.*

He seemed more interested in talking about himself.

The surgeon seemed to do a good job but I never saw him again. I had some questions to ask him.

I'd have tension headaches, too, if I had a wife like yours (in the presence of the wife).

Oh, you're right. I was suppose to call you last week about your breast biopsy. I'll check into it and call you Monday.

My wife had CTs 2 weeks ago to check the status of her cancer after chemotherapy. After 4 or 5 phone calls the only response we got was a fax of the CT reports which showed enlarging and new metastases!

The neurologist called us and said the head CT on grandpa showed a brain stem infarction and 'he will probably die within 24 hours'. The neurologist hadn't yet seen the patient who was up walking around and conversing.

You're just depressed—snap out of it.

You're a walking plaque.

There is nothing more I can do for you; you know you brought this on yourself.

We don't know who my doctor is here in the hospital.

♦ **You will have many opportunities to be quiet and not speak; you should take advantage of each of these!** (RA Lee)

My doctor is not as sympathetic as I'd like him to be.

I left my doctor's office feeling worse than when I came in.

He wouldn't return my phone calls.

Kept me waiting then spent most of the time on the phone.

The following is from physicians as patients, or family of physicians or patients, who published their anguished experiences in leading medical journals, and not just letters to the editors.

She received treatments, medicines, and procedures, but no care at the end.

Surgical attendings just don't have time to talk to families, the nurses explained apologetically to the patient's two physician sons.

Without introducing herself, the physician began to wonder out loud why Jerry would want to "kill your mother by stopping dialysis. Maybe to get her out of your hair, huh?"

From another physician: I've been unlucky on many occasions in not receiving optimum care.

As I (a professor of surgery) watched my oldest daughter die of cancer for 4 long years, I sensed and experienced the tension between hope and acknowledgment. When hope can be only false hope and when failure to acknowledge the threat of death becomes a form of abandonment. I learned that an appointment broken or canceled, or the unannounced substitution of another consultant, was to my daughter, who was a nurse, a very specific form of abandonment. "Dad, they are giving up on me."

From another professor of surgery in his own hospital about his father-in-law's end-of- life care: His final days might have been much less unpleasant and trying for him and his family. His physicians were little more than technicians, ordering tests and prescribing treatments. There was little explanation of the tests ordered. Nobody discussed intubation or dialysis with him. Even after our family chose to withdraw all treatment and let nature take its course, the housestaff dutifully continued to order x-ray studies.

I ask, "Where was the attending staff all this time? Why weren't they teaching the housestaff about end-of-life issues and reigning in some control on tests ordered?"

> A patient publishes her experience in an emergency department where she presented with vaginal bleeding where the resident said in front of the patient to a medical student: *This bitch thought that by inducing vaginal bleeding with a corrosive, she might trick me into thinking it was cervical bleeding. Then I'd perform a D and C and she'd have her abortion!*
>
> From another article in a major medical journal: *I notice the nurses in his office mirror his attitude...arrogant...aloof...superior...after all, they are the attendants to a star. "You are lucky. Be happy he made time for you at all".* Is this not the epitome of pomposity or what!
>
> From a letter to the editor in the New York Times (a source of a lot of my material: *"...while in the hospital having a knee replacement, I asked the nurse when she thought I would go home. Without missing a beat, the nurse replied, 'Knees go home after four days'. I remember feeling so hurt and angry. I had an instant image in my head that I was a knee, sitting in my wheelchair, not a person but a body part. It is a very painful memory."*

> ♦ **How great some men would be if they weren't arrogant!** (the Talmud)

> About an oncologist: *He didn't seem interested in me. I didn't go back.*

To many people, and not just in the patient-physician interaction, indifference is a greater hurt than dislike or even hate. The latter can be dealt with, whereas indifference gives you the sense that you are not really a being; you're almost non existent.

> *He was there all of ...maybe 3 minutes. Later, the bill comes for my comprehensive examination--$500!*
>
> *What bothers me, besides the money, is the attitude. The physicians, the nurses, and the hospital couldn't have cared less about me.*
>
> *My doctor is nice; every time I see him I'm ashamed of what I think of doctors in general.*
>
> *I simply couldn't warm up to him.*
>
> *I just wish he would brood over me.*
>
> *His "good morning" had an automatic quality. He was aware that I was a physician but knew nothing else about me and made it clear that he had no further interest. He addressed the medical students on the 'classic' findings of ALS (Lou Gehrig's disease) [per the electromyogram]. He positively bubbled with joy at finding even more evidence of the sickened state of my motor neurons. How often do we treat our patients this way? What did that teach those young students about the importance of empathy and compassion? Callousness. Dr L., the antithesis of caring, could become common as medical care becomes more fragmented and long term relationships with patients become relics. Physicians are the vital human link that can give patients the strength they require. As the pace of medicine quickens, physicians who teach will bear special responsibility to provide strong examples of empathy and professionalism to students and residents. After all, one day we may all find ourselves on the other side of the bed rail, and those young physicians will become what we model for them today.* **AMEN!**

The amen is my added exclamation. This physician summarized the potential state of affairs beautifully. The lack of role models and mentors is a sorry state. I'm always intrigued how some physicians poorly treat other physicians; I can't imagine how they treat a 'stranger', the vulnerable patient.

These are examples of 'compassion fatigue' on the part of physicians and nurses. Maybe they were never compassionate and should have been weeded out much earlier while still in training. But to give them benefit of the doubt, they have lost it! Signs of impending compassion fatigue/burnout are belittling remarks about patients, anger towards patients and their families, feeling imposed upon by the patients and the whole medical system, and total lack of mindfulness as to how their emotions are affecting their interactions with patients. Ideally, a valued allied health staff/nurse would tell the physician how she perceives him, at the peril of losing her job. But losing her job might be the best thing to happen to her at this point rather than working with a physician of this caliber.

♦ **He had delusions of adequacy!** (Walter Kerr)

There seems to be a common theme in many of these physician comments to patients and that is one of anger and arrogance, over and above lack of compassion and empathy—they just don't care. How would they feel if a physician spoke to one of their family members that way! Or themselves!!!

Does anger really ever accomplish anything? The comments I've recorded completely take away hope, making it that much harder for other physicians to restore it. I think with patients and peers (peers hear about these 'cringe words' comments from their patients like I did) someday grading physicians, they will grade the offending physician accordingly. How much damage will they do before this happens? These physicians may be forced into anger management courses by the hospital practice board, as these arrogant comments are a precursor to lawsuits.

In spite of the importance of nonverbal communication, how we manage verbal communication is extremely important. It can do far more long lasting hurt and mistrust in a few moments than your nonverbal body language.

Words should be measured as the patient will remember what they want to hear and not uncommonly out of the context in which the physician intended. You can be sure that many of these patients will pass on these negative connotations to whoever will listen. Or, maybe put them on the Internet!

♦ **It's not what's said, it's what's heard!**

This is so true. I'm repeating this because it is so true in life, not just in medicine. Over the years when I have seen patients on a return visit some time later, and I've been impressed that the patient didn't fully understand what I said, so since I am in a referral center and wrote a letter to every home physician, I always included a copy to the patient and asked them to be sure I was correct. If, for some reason there wasn't a physician to write to, I almost always sent a summary to the patient and told them to make copies to give to the home physician, when necessary, and always keep a copy in their health file. This is not usually possible in a primary care setting but it serves to make a point.

Some years ago a patient taught me a good lesson. He was in his 70s and pretty healthy. He came to the Clinic for a general exam and a reassessment of his hypertension and moderate osteoarthritic symptoms. I thoroughly examined him and performed some routine laboratory tests and told him things looked good after going over all the results with him. A week later his son called me and told me his dad was down in the dumps and concerned about his cancer (which he didn't have)—he was certain that he had a cancer because I didn't specifically tell him he did not have one!

Overcoming misperceptions isn't easy. You will maybe recall the adage that a negative comment to a child can take up to 5 or more positive comments by the perpetrator to regain the lost self-esteem and confidence. Are vulnerable adults any different? We must learn to manage the perceptions to make sure they are accurate.

Every physician must develop their own words and manner of conveying bad news, hopefully from good role models as well as words they'd like to hear if the situation were reversed. But the exact words aren't as important as the tone in which they are delivered—with empathy, sincerity, genuineness. And the 2 words *I'm sorry* are not only empathetic, but the physician, and any person, saying them begins to feel an empathy, if he or she doesn't already, by just saying them. I can't repeat often enough the importance of these 2 words in their appropriate context, not just in the patient-physician encounter, but in all walks of life.

♦ Talk to me, not at me!

The most important aspect of verbal communication is the need and the ability to **listen**. This is true in all aspects of human interaction, not just in medicine. *Listening is the sincerest form of flattery.* It also shows respect to the person talking. We have 2 ears and 1 mouth for good reason and they should be used accordingly.

It's as important to know how to Listen as when to listen!

I can't stress this enough, and this becomes even more important when dealing with the difficult patient which I'll discuss later. This is true in life, not just the physician-patient interaction. *You need to be listening for what isn't being said!*

♦ The best way to entertain some folk is to let them do all the talking, especially about themselves!

I like to refer to genuine listening as 'deep' or 'reflective' listening and this is done without prejudice, judgment, preconceived notions, or negative feelings. This is *being present in the moment for the patient. Mindfulness!* You can't let your personal problems interfere with your work. Never take your anger to work *with you!*

Stephen Covey lists 'empathetic listening' (what I call deep or reflective listening) as Habit #5 in his book *The 7 Habits of Highly Effective People* and describes this as 'listening with the intention to understand'. Most people listen with the intent to reply, to give their opinion, rather than to understand. Covey points out that empathetic or reflective listening takes time but not nearly as much time as it takes to back up and correct misunderstandings. *Listening is how I experience you.*

♦ You must listen, not just hear!

Effective listening is a learned skill that comes from discipline. Listening is extremely therapeutic; the patient feels that you are taking them seriously. It also gives them a sense of control and at the same time, a sense of dignity. The physician can't express empathy and establish trust without listening. It builds trust. In a study published in the *New England Journal of Medicine* by Levinson a few years ago timed a group of surgeons spent with patients. The surgeons who spent an average of only 3 more minutes with patients were almost never sued, whereas, those who spent the shorter times with patients were not uncommonly sued and had more dissatisfied patients. I'm sure that the extra time taken by the competent surgeons was because he or she was listening more.

> ♦ **Listen with your eyes, listen for feelings!**

It requires the mindfulness of being present in the moment, not thinking about other things while listening to the patient. You *must want to listen*, and this is always done by maintaining eye contact, not looking out the window or at the computer screen. And you try not to interrupt. Allow the patient to talk for the first 2 or 3 minutes uninterrupted, even if they wander. The patient will think they have been talking for at least 10 minutes. It has been shown that the physician interrupts roughly every 20 seconds. This justifies the statement "...that he never listens to me." *You can't learn anything while you're talking*.

> ♦ **The best way to talk to a teenager is to listen!**

While listening it is appropriate to respond with facial expressions and nodding of the head that reflect your reception of the signals from the talker, along with "Uh-huh," "Yes," "I understand," "Go on," "Tell me about it," and so on. These are usually spontaneous if you are really attuned to listening. Too much silence can be interpreted as disinterest.

> **I think that's the secret to listening—**
> **To realize the other person isn't really looking for an answer.**
> **They're interested in empathy, sensitivity, and understanding!**
> **Father Andrew Greely**

It's probable that many people go to a doctor for just the reason Father Greely mentions—to find someone to listen to them, not for answers.

As stated earlier the only appropriate time to frown is when empathizing with a patient's suffering. Good listening may be a gift for some but a relatively easily acquired virtue by others, providing they want to listen.

> **Sincerity is key to this whole business...**
> **...once you learn to fake that you have it made!**
> **Monte Clark**
> **NFL coach**

Sincerity may require tact—mix kindness with the truth when you tell it. Listening is therapeutic and empathetic. It is therapeutic to know someone is truly listening to you and therapeutic because just ventilating, talking about something or someone bothering you, can significantly release pent up tensions. It is a partial transference of problems to an interested person, the relief that someone is sharing your hurts. It is also time consuming in the midst of a busy schedule but necessary for establishing trust.

If you don't feel you're being listened to,
You don't feel you're being listened to!

This is especially true for the difficult patient (see below).

Many patients are reluctant to express their emotions and innermost concerns, especially to a 'stranger' they haven't yet established a trust with and this is particularly true with men. The physician needs to read the body language of the patient as he or she is speaking and in subtle ways encourage them to open up. This may not be easy. Comments at the end of the interview like, "Is there anything else you want to talk about that I should know so I can help you?" or, "What questions can I answer for you?" (this is the better way to phrase it than "Do you have any questions?") allows the patient to realize that you are interested in them. But it may not be until the next visit or two that they open up. It may be then that they decided to discuss their depression you've inquired about in previous visits. If a patient cancels or doesn't show for appointments, it may be a sign he or she isn't up to talking about something then. Or, if they know you are going to scold them again, they may be thinking about going to another physician.

♦ **Listening well is often silent but never passive!** (MP Nichols)

Even if you know what someone is going to say, you need to let them say it and acknowledge it. Don't interrupt.

♦ **Don't listen to what I say; listen to what I mean!** (Father Andrew Greely)

As you listen, comprehend what the patient is describing as if it is coming from the whole person, not the diseased organ such as the emphysematous lung that is causing shortness of breath, or the atherosclerotic coronary artery disease of the heart that is causing chest pain. The patient is almost certainly trying to tell you how the disease is affecting their soul, their being, not just the organ—listen! Your listening and your eye contact is likened to 'soul to soul' communication.

♦ **Don't jump to respond—listen harder!** (MP Nichols)

You might call this 'aerobic' listening. When dealing with the difficult patient, listening is the most important thing you can do. I'll discuss my thoughts on this in the section on patient-physician interaction.

Nichols' book on *The Lost Art of Listening* has to do mostly with personal relationships but he has a number of messages that apply to the patient-physician interactions that I've outlined below.

- When we see sadness or depression in someone, we tend to assume that something's wrong, that something has happened. Maybe that something is that nobody's listening.
- Some people have no idea how pressured and provoking their tone of voice is, but they come at you like a bad dentist.

- The reason we don't recognize the impact of the tone of our own voice is that the listener hears what the speaker feels like, not what we sound like.
- Listening is the art by which we use empathy to reach across the space between us. Passive attention won't work.
- There's a big difference between showing interest and really taking interest.
- Listening can be perceived by the listener as a loss of control. Actually, with appropriate listening you gain a sense of control—you understand, and the speaker senses this.
- We only hear what we want to hear.

No one explained to me what they meant by zero tolerance!
Bobby Knight
U of Indiana basketball
coach on his firing

Communication involves more than mere words...
They want to be looked after and not just looked
Over...to be listened to...they want to feel that
It makes a difference to the physician whether they live
Or die. They want to feel that they
Are in the physician's thoughts!
Normal Cousins

Touching, the right kind of touching can be powerful but its mechanism is not understood. As mentioned in the section on the science of caring, hugging raises the levels of oxytoxin which is beneficial. What happens when the physician professionally touches the patient besides enhancing bonding? Something happens. In pet therapy we know that when a person pets an animal, it can lower high blood pressure, slow the pulse and respiratory rate and ease muscle tension.

And always find a way to touch the patient, with what is called 'professional touching'. Shaking hands and looking them in the eye is the most obvious; or a hand on the shoulder during part of the exam. It gives the patient a confidence in her physician. Many people don't like to be touched, that is, until they become sick or worried, then they need *caring touch.* It is necessary for compassion, it has some positive effects on the immune system, and it contributes to serenity. Rest your hand on their forearm if they are bedfast and leave it there a bit.

An interesting study was done where young people in a café were observed over a pre-determined period of time and the number of times they touched each other. The results were as follows: London, none; Orlando 2 times; Paris 110 times and San Juan 180 times. Teenagers from the last 2 cities are much less aggressive than those from the first two.

A loving spouse's touch on someone who is dying produces a greater calming effect than someone else's touch such as a nurse, even though the spouse hasn't spoken! How does the patient know it is his or her spouse? What "message" is transmitted via the touch? And where in the brain is it received? And then passed on to where else in the brain to produce the calming effect?

A letter from a Mayo cancer patient: *I had not realized the value of touch until I experienced the stress that goes with a cancer diagnosis and surgery. Thank you for taking care of me physically and mentally.*

◆ **The skin craves to be touched!**

There is a phenomena in Eastern European countries where newborns wait to be adopted and while doing so are almost never held by anyone. This occurs over many months and sometimes years. They are 'sterile', emotionless. Later in life they are devoid of establishing interpersonal relationships.

I suspect that *caring touch* is much more powerful than we can imagine, especially when given with a smile, and if appropriate, some calming words. I suspect the toucher (the physician, health care personnel, family, friends, or mutual friends unrelated to illness) benefit from the touch, just as does the touchee. We physicians should capitalize on this whenever we can. In my early days it was usual for nurses to give back rubs to patients; now they are too busy for this. We've lost a chance to accelerate the healing process.

Hug your kids every chance you can. As I think about this I think this is a two way street—I benefit by the touch even though I initiated it. Wouldn't it be reasonable advice to your teenagers to not marry anyone who doesn't like to be hugged?

THE PATIENT-PHYSICIAN INTERACTION

The patient-physician encounter sets the stage for the healing process, but it must be in the form of a partnership built on mutual trust. This can occur with a one-time visit such as occurs in a subspecialty consultation, but it usually takes a few visits, with the same doctor, for trust to be firmly established (or lost). It can't be limited to a one-way interaction from the physician to the patient. The patient must be actively involved in this relationship including the decision making. It has only been the last several decades where an individual went to his or her physician without any complaints for a general exam and advice on preventive medicine measures. And for peace of mind that all is OK. Frequently this was (or is) done to establish a relationship with a care giver "...who will be there when I need him or her."

> ♦ **A patient new to a physician doesn't care as much about how much the physician knows until she knows how much the physician cares!**

The patient-physician interaction/partnership relates strongly to the patient's well-being. It is principally because this relationship has become so strained that trust has been lost, not only with the physician but also with the whole health care system. I have spent a lot of time gathering facts I have learned in my nearly 50 years in medicine including observations of my role models and mentors, and dealing with tens of thousands of patients.

With a partnership the physician is trying to respect the patient's autonomy, but there may need to be a gentle push-pull between the patient and the doctor (often nonverbal) to allow the doctor to try to decide how much autonomy the patient really wants. The concept of loss of control on the part of the patient can't be underestimated. The struggle for control can be very stressful and is inversely proportional to the trust and comfort with the physician(s) and the health care team by the patient and the family.

> ♦ **Research shows that the patient-physician relationship is the most consistently reported determinant for <u>physician</u> satisfaction!**

In regard to the physician's role in the partnership, I refer below to these pearls as 'the little things' that I wish I knew as a young physician, but as is true of life, you learn by experience, from role models, and if you are fortunate, mentors. By putting these together I hope I can save the young physician from learning some of these things the hard way and contribute to the joy of the practice of the Art of Medicine. I also hope that the 'patient' reading these will learn what I think the ideal patient-physician interaction should be. I've alluded to a number of these already but they are worth repeating.

Being a patient in the best of hands, in the best of situations, can still be a humiliating experience. We, the health care team, must minimize this, while at the same time, accept this. Oftentimes, it isn't until the physician him or herself becomes a patient with a problem that he appreciates the humility of what their patient feels. If a medical student has never been a patient in a hospital, they should be admitted overnight to experience what their patients do. Go down a long hallway and on an elevator while lying flat on your back with others 'looking down' on you. You won't forget this!

The Little Things in the Practice of the Art of Medicine by the Physician, or,
How to be a Physician!

- You will never go wrong if you practice the *Platinum Rule of Medicine*, which is to take care of the patient like you would want a member of your family cared for. Patients deserve to be treated like family. If you do this always, you can skip this section of the book.

  ♦ **The average person is more interested in his or her own name than all the other names on earth put together!** (Dale Carnegie)

- Begin by always saying the patient's name, by the name they wish to be called, and repeat this every so often. This personalizes the encounter, and is good in practicing the Art of Living as well. The older I get the more I appreciate the absolute importance of greeting all people I know by their name. The person takes this as a very personal compliment, that you cared enough to call them by their name. For the patient it establishes the power of caring right off. I am a believer that you don't call a patient by their first name unless they are under 25 years old, and if the patient insisted in being called by their 1st name, I insisted they call me by my first name; this happens when your patient becomes a personal friend which is often. But if they are considerably senior, I always called them Mr or Mrs or Miss and always with the nursing home patient (unless they call me by my first name). This allows the nursing home patient to maintain some dignity, which they have lost considerably because of where they are. The nurses, nurse's aid, and your office staff should follow these rules. Never use the words "Dearie", "Honey", etc. This is *respect*. And remember, the patient and the family will judge you within the first five seconds of your encounter with them.
- Be on time. Of course, not always possible but have your office staff tell the patient why you are late and do so every so often. Or, you stick your head in the room and let them know you are coming soon. And apologize for being late. Being on time is analogous to airline punctuality—if the plane is on time, no one complains about the service, the food, the baggage mishandling. But the more delays there are, they'll complain about everything. The patient's time is important, too.
- When entering the patient's room, if the door is closed, gently knock first.
- Ask what are their expectations for today's visit.
- If you are seeing them for the first time, be sure they know your name and why you are seeing them.
- Words like, *How can I help you?* are very meaningful and begin the process of bonding and trust. Even if this is the only time you will see them for this problem, establishing trust gives the patient a sense of trust, not just in you, but in the whole medical system. It is one of your obligations. Other worthy phrases are *Don't hesitate to get in touch with me any time,* or, *Call me at home,* and *We are going to take good care of you.* Your office personnel must also make the patient feel that they are important to them as well.

**There is a miraculous moment
When the very presence of the doctor
Is the most effective part of the treatment!**
Rene Dubos

- A moment of small talk also helps. "How are the kids, your husband?" "Did you go on the vacation we talked about last time?" Occasionally there is a place to tell the patient what you have been doing, but don't talk about yourself too much. If the patient bonds with you, however, they will want to know something about you.
- Ultimately find a way to compliment the patient—how they look, how well they did with the instructions you gave them, about their weight reduction. Empathize you know how hard they've struggled with their disease. This is very important!
- Ask how their illness is affecting them, and their family.
- Availability of appointments can be a frustration to patients, especially if you are a good doctor! You may have to limit your practice in order to give good continuity of care.

Three things in human life are important.
The first is to be kind, the second is to be kind, and
The third is to be kind!
Henry James

- Kindness, being nice. As I've said earlier, you don't need to define these terms, you know it when you see it, or, worse, when you don't see it. Body language expresses this. Similar human characteristics are 'warmth', 'respect', 'caring with dignity', 'empathetic'. These should be there for every patient, every day, no matter how your day is going. Practice being a little kinder than necessary, to everyone. *And be kind and gentle with yourself.*

- ◆ **Wherever there is a human being, there is an opportunity for kindness!**

Kindness says, "I just want you to be happier!"
- Equanimity!
- Don't hesitate to unmask a depression. Up to 25% of your patients will be depressed. Studies have shown that the patient with an undiagnosed mental problem (most often a depression) averages nearly a dozen office visits a year before the diagnosis and treatment versus only 4 the next year, a real burden to health care costs and your time and frustration. Even the costs in the hospitalized patient are considerably greater. If your time with the patient is too limited to get into the possibility of whether or not they are depressed, reschedule a visit soon. But tell the patient that you are going to help them and reassure them that mental illness is slowly becoming 'an accepted disorder', it is nothing to be ashamed about. In the interval they can think about this and maybe be more open with you.
- Appear relaxed. Sit down—shouldn't have to mention this, but I've heard of many physicians who stand to give reports to the patient so that they can get out of the room that much quicker! This is rude and arrogant. Sit down! And listen! The patient will estimate that they spent twice as much time with you as they actually did and be much more satisfied.
- Body language. You may have to think about this. The patient is reading this constantly and maybe getting the wrong signals from you. Your body language will accomplish a lot for you if you let it, and ultimately save you time. Smile! Eye contact! Listen! Don't interrupt! We've been over this before. It's about your attitude!

- Professionally touch the patient—hand shake, arm around the shoulder, 'laying on the hands on the patient in bed.'
- Can you feel if the patient is comfortable with you? Do you think they feel rushed? Do they feel you are doing your best?
- Don't look at your watch. If you need to know the time, place a wall or desk clock behind the patient, or on your desk between you and the patient.
- Your exam of the patient should be appropriately thorough. Wash your hands in front of the patient. Explain what you are going to do. Respect modesty with appropriate covering. Be gentle. Be sure your breath is fresh and don't chew gum. Try to avoid words like 'hurt' and 'pain' as these lower the patient's pain threshold. 'Discomfort' is more acceptable. This is especially true when doing a procedure on the patient. During or immediately after the exam explain your findings including the normal ones and always give them the blood pressure results.

♦ **You can't heal if you are angry!**

- Never get angry with the patient or family (or the health care personnel, or anyone!). And never argue with the patient; disagreements can be handled in a calm, reassuring manner. With equanimity! And as I have said earlier, *never take your anger to work with you*—deal with it! A psychiatrist will tell you that the problem with dealing with your anger is that you'll eventually have to deal with what is the source of the anger. Unresolved anger becomes 'swallowed anger' and leads to more stress, a compromise of your values, and even physical ailments. I'm impressed how much anger there is all around. Chronic anger leads to hatred—can you afford this!!! The angry person engenders very little respect.

♦ **Let there be peace on earth and let it begin with me!** (Methodist hymn)

- Never criticize another physician to the patient or the house staff, and never, never put this in writing.
- Use great caution in disagreeing with the diagnosis of another physician. You may be correct but it can really confuse the patient. There is a right way to do this. Try to find a way to compliment the patient's physician, if you are not the primary physician.
- Never hesitate to say, *I'm sorry.*
- Avoid talking about patients in elevators, hallways, etc. This is a no-brainer, but it happens all the time. Also use caution in laughter in the hallways where very sick and even terminally ill patients can hear it. This is inappropriate.
- Never use terms like 'GOMER'(Get Out of My ER), 'a Hit', 'PMS' (Poor Miserable Sap) or refer to a patient by a diagnosis—'the brain tumor down the hall'. And don't tolerate anyone else using these terms, ever. It undermines the culture of an institution.
- Ask yourself, "Am I arrogant?" or "Perceived as being arrogant?"

♦ **From a surgeon to his son going into surgical practice: Never operate on a stranger!** (RA Lee)

- Always maintain tolerance for diversity; without it you are, by definition, arrogant. It isn't so much a matter of tolerating differences in behaviors, race, religion, etc; it's accepting that *it can't be any other way*. The opposite of intolerance is understanding. Tolerance can have a negative impact in that if you accept someone's differences but then because of the differences you don't want any part of them hurts almost as much as intolerance.

- Never talk down to the patient. Explain things in a language they can understand. Avoid medical jargon, even if the patient uses medical terms. Write down the names of the diagnoses for them, especially if it is something brand new to them. And ask the patient or the family member to repeat back to you instructions you have given them. What may seem simple to you may be very complicated for them, especially if there is a language barrier or limited education. Take advantage of a health educator.
- Include the family, if the patient wishes. May save you some time.
- Return phone calls promptly. This is integrity.
- What is the tone of your voice on the phone? Does it sound like the patient is interfering with your busy day? If you smile when answering the phone, the caller can 'see' it.
- Discuss options. Allow the patient to be involved in the decision making. Empowering the patient to partner with you in their care is <u>very</u> important. However, many patients will have established great trust in you to the point that they want you to make all the decisions. Even so, you need to get their input and approval of your decisions and make sure they understand. If your decisions are major ones, repeat them to the patient and family. Then ask what questions you can answer for them; this is more open than asking "Do you have any questions?"
- Guide the workup of the patient, depending on the potential seriousness and the patient's anxiety. Their time is important, also. Expedite their tests and the reporting of the results to them. No woman should have to wait more than 24 hours for a mammogram result; she has a mammogram for one reason only—to rule out cancer.

The convenience of the patient must take Precedence
Over the convenience of the health care team!
Don Berwick

- After going over the laboratory results with the patient, give them a copy (with the normal values) and tell them to put it in their own medical file. If they are someday seeing another physician for any reason, remind them to always take their health file with them.
- You may have seen hundreds of patients with breast cancer, but as far as the patient is concerned, this is her first breast cancer. *Every patient is the only patient.*
- Keep a tickler file of all your patients who are undergoing a workup with their phone number and e-mail address and you or your trusted office employee check on test results at the end of each day. E-mail the normal or negative results and you personally call the patient with abnormal or sensitive test results. You care. Turns out that in over 40% of hospitalized patients, the results of some of their tests don't become available until after discharge. And a fair percent of these require some urgent action, providing you are aware of the delayed results!

- ◆ **A close relationship between the patient and you may not be valuable to you but can be absolutely priceless to the patient!** (Thomas J Watson Jr, former IBM CEO and Mayo Trustee)

- Keep up with the science. Through the Internet your patient may come back to you with the correct diagnosis! And know more about their disease than you do. Accept this. This is maturity.

**Ultimately it is the physician's respect for the
Human soul that determines the
Worth of his science!**
Raul Raod

- ♦ **Three former Master's golf champions were told "...your play no longer is deemed up to Master's standards!"**

- Never tell the patient there is nothing more you can do. Do Something! This might be as simple as saying, "Let's sit tight and see you again in a few weeks or few months and recheck, or, call me in a few weeks to update me." Or, try a medication you know is harmless and see what happens. *Placebos are powerful;* this can be seen on functional MRIs. Is the patient depressed as a cause of their unexplained symptoms? Tricyclic antidepressants work on some symptoms in the non depressed patient like peripheral neuropathies, but these aren't without some side effects. Behavior modification also works!
- If you are on the staff in an academic medical center and have the hospital service, you are the physician of record. You must be sure that the patient is getting the best possible care. Consider going back after rounds to see the patient without the house staff (or just the resident in charge) to clarify some things. This is extremely important if things not going as well as expected. This doesn't undermine the experience of the residents; on the contrary, it will teach them a lot. You are the role model. Be sure the patient has the written names of all the physicians taking care of them.

**Is there anything more doleful
Than three or four physicians entering a patient's room!**
Sir William Osler

- Never tell an off-color story in mixed company, and never use foul language—this is character.
- Finally, ask, again, *What questions can I answer for you?*

- ♦ **An unsolicited phone call from you, as the credit-card ad goes, is "priceless". This is a tremendous act of bonding. The same goes for a house call. You care!**

How to be a Patient—the Patient's Half of the Partnership

You might also call this The Art of Being a Patient. As physicians I think we have an obligation to teach our patients how to visit the doctor. Ideally, this should begin in health classes in schools but I wouldn't count on it. It's not the patients' fault that they don't know how. An orderly, succinct, well thought out presentation by the patient for the reasons they come to see the doctor can smooth the patient-physician encounter and ultimately lead to better patient compliance. It certainly will reduce some of the physician's frustrations, as this has been shown to be a source of friction with some physicians. The history given by the patient, the 'interview', is perhaps the most important aspect of this encounter.

If we can teach you, the patient, the type of information we need, and teach you how to present your history, leaving out the extraneous side events like, "I think my problem began the day we went to visit Aunt Minnie, or, was it the day before that?" "Let me think now," will make the presentation almost like a rehearsal. In fact, rehearsing what you are going to say either to yourself or with a family member will help you and your doctor greatly. It will help clarify in your mind what is going on. You will come away from the physician visit with a feeling of some control over your health care and overall have a better feeling about the quality of the visit. The physician will see that you are truly interested in your health (sometimes we physicians get the feeling that the patient isn't interested, at least not until things don't seem to be getting better).

◆ **Patients should be encouraged in responsible participation!**

The day is gone when a visit to the doctor is part social, part 'business'. The name of the game now is TIME. One of the most common complaints by the patient is, "He never seemed to have enough time to spend with me." The next most common is, "She didn't communicate with me". These two are usually interrelated and not uncommonly because not enough time is available within the 10 or 15 minutes allotted by the 3rd party payers. Learning how to present a series of related symptoms chronologically as they occurred greatly improves the efficiency of the visit.

To begin with you need to think this out ahead of the visit, why you are going to see the doctor, and what are your expectations. Some patients tend to put the most important concern they have part way down their list or save it until last. It should be first. You should include a written list in non-sentence format of the time sequence of the events, a sort of diary. I'm not talking about routine office visits to get a blood pressure or blood sugar check, but for when you go to the doctor with a complaint that doesn't have a clear meaning to you and you want some relief and reassurance.

You need to be aware that the physician's time is increasingly consumed by paper work, meetings devoted to learning how to conform to federal regulations, time spent to get permission for more tests or referrals for a patient, and frustrated patients wanting to by-pass an office visit and do medicine only by phone or e-mail. This leaves less time for families, exercise, hobbies and other diversions and keeping up with the science of medicine at conferences or reading the medical literature. These pressures are causing physicians to retire 'prematurely', or go into administration, leaving less experienced physicians in the practice of medicine.

Too great of expectations by the patient of what the physician or the science of medicine can do is a major frustration to physicians and this is because of what you read in the newspapers or see on TV. When a report comes out that there may be a cure for cancer, the news reporter doesn't mention that it might be another 10 years before it is available. And too often patients abuse themselves by not exercising, not controlling their weight, smoking, not taking their medications and then expecting their doctor to straighten everything out.

I mention all this because as a partner in your care you need to know some of the other side of what is happening. I have always felt that our best ally is our patients, well informed patients. The 3rd party payers and government health administrators rarely do anything to make the patient-physician encounter more precious. They are only interested in the bottom line.

Once in the doctor's office it is almost too late to try to sort out a complicated problem. Too often, the spouse (usually the wife) will pop up and say, "...you've got it all wrong, your abdominal pain began 3 weeks ago and your fever 1 week ago, and you did have chills!" And never turn to the spouse (again, almost always the husband to the wife in my experience) and ask her, "Where was my chest pain?", or, "How long did it last?", "Was it sharp or dull?" I am a firm believer that unless the patient is incompetent that it is his and his alone responsibility to know his medical history. Know where the chest pain was, how long it lasted, the nature of it, were there any precipitating factors like exercise, etc! You must take control of your health, including being involved with major decisions. This is *patient autonomy,* an ownership of your health.

One aspect to ownership is knowing when to apply an appropriate amount of assertiveness. But you must approach the patient-doctor interaction with an open mind rather than already having your mind made up as to what is wrong with you and what is to be done about it.

You should have a ready answer for every thing the doctor asks, rather than say "...well, let me see now, I'm not sure what came first," or, "I don't remember if I was short of breath with the chest pain or not." "I'm trying to think, did the symptoms occur before or after eating," or, "I don't know what medicines I'm on, I've been to so many different doctors!" The physician isn't a magician and if it takes many minutes to sort this out in an allotted 10 minute office visit, extremely valuable time has been lost. And the patients in the waiting room will wonder, again, why they have to wait for the doctor, just as you have many times in the past!

Another problem we encounter is your perception of time in the past. We might ask you when you pain began and how long it lasted and we want to know in terms of seconds, minutes, hours, days, weeks, months and years! To answer, "A while back," or, "Sometime ago," "A while ago," "Not very long," doesn't mean anything to us. Not having the specifics available in your mind and on paper only slows down the interview. You need to think this out ahead and write it down.

If you have medical records from other physicians, bring them in, preferably in the order of their dates. And bring in all medications, in their original bottle, including over the counter (OTC) medications, herbal medicines, and eye drops, unless you were in her office recently for similar problems and no new medications have been added or deleted in the interval. The drugs you bring in includes drugs you received from other physicians. And even though you bring them in, you should also have them on a list you keep in your purse or wallet and update it accordingly any time there is a change. Complications of drugs, including OTC drugs and interactions with other drugs, are one of the biggest and more serious problems we (the patient and the physician) face. Just because a drug is heavily advertised doesn't necessarily mean it is any better than alternative, less expensive, safer drugs. Or that OTC drugs and herbal medicines are always safe because you don't need a doctor's prescription to get them.

Use caution on asking for (demanding?) certain tests or drugs that your doctor feels are unnecessary. Physicians can usually tell which drugs have been blitzed-advertised on TV. There is great concern now that overuse of antibiotics is dramatically causing a rise in antibiotic resistant bacteria that we have no alternative antibiotics for. Usual antibiotics do not work on viruses such as the flu or common cold. But many a busy physician finds 'it easier to prescribe an antibiotic than argue with a patient who demands it.'

Again, a lot of what I have said depends on whether this is a 'routine' office visit for a blood pressure or blood test recheck, or prescription refill, or if it is a problem the patient wishes to address with the physician. If in doubt, come prepared!

Please keep your appointment or cancel it so that another patient can be worked in. You wouldn't no-show for tee-off time or a hair appointment.

Take your medicine as prescribed and for the full course. If you can't afford it, tell your pharmacist and your doctor—maybe there is a less expensive alternative.

The patient should not be offering diagnoses with the symptoms as this confuses things, but ultimately your doctor, if he or she isn't sure of what is going on after the initial visit, should ask you what you think.

Eventually, at least 25% of the population will be significantly depressed; it can manifest different ways over and above feeling sad. It might be the cause of insomnia, back or abdominal pain, headaches, loss of interest in socializing and many more. The patient is looking for a disease-cause of their symptoms. If there is the slightest chance you are depressed, mention this to your physician, as many physicians are reluctant to 'unmask' a depression because it can be very time consuming if you are trying to avoid admitting to it. However, ultimately it will save hours of time and multiple office visits and probably many tests if it is diagnosed and treated.

In the 'old days' the diagnosis of a mental illness carried tremendous stigmata, certainly for men whose macho image couldn't handle it. And in the old days, you were usually referred to a psychiatrist, where the patient has images of being in a locked ward or spending time on the couch talking about his childhood. Now the medications for most depressions are great and very effective and usually only needed for 6 to 12 months, not a lifetime. Ask yourself, "...are my symptoms possibly due to depression?" You don't need a reason to be depressed—it results from a chemical change in the brain. Don't fight it!

Your time can be as valuable as the doctor's and now most physicians are trying to stay on time, but you also know that acute illnesses don't follow a clock (and babies come when they want to) and that your doctor almost always doesn't have an opening on any one day to squeeze you in, unless it is built into the schedule and for the busy physician this is hard to do. As a result of having to work these patients in, he or she may be delayed getting to you.

The time constraints are because of 3rd party payers who pay only a finite amount per standard office visit. And the physician has a tremendous office and professional overhead.

It is not necessary to remind you that you aren't the only patient the physician has and that on some days he or she sees numerous patients with very challenging medical as well as social and mental problems. These are difficult if not impossible to handle in the 10 minutes allotted. These challenges plus the time constraints are very stressful to the physician, especially the compassionate physician who carries many of these burdens on his or her shoulders and takes them home with her.

117

For all these reasons, and more, it is all the more important for you, and maybe your family, to try to make the visit with the physician as smooth and 'business-like' as possible, but not so business-like that it discourages bonding.

When your doctor returns your phone call, know exactly what you want answered. This is not the time to ask him or her about your sister-in-law's or your neighbor's symptoms. She may have 10 or more calls to make and it is 6 o'clock.

You, the patient, may not realize that it is almost as important that the patient allow the physician to establish some trust with you, just as you do with the physician. If the physician can't trust you to be interested in getting better, in being honest with the facts, in complying with recommendations, the physician loses some interest, maybe total interest. In fact, physician overall satisfaction correlates with the patient's adherence to his or her recommendations as well as with the patient's satisfaction. The mutual trust will be gone.

> ♦ **Studies consistently show that the patient-physician relationship is the most consistently reported as the main determinant of physician satisfaction!**

Listen to the physician. I've noted a number of times that the patient's mind is wandering and not listening to a thing that is being said. In fact, they interrupt with an irrelevant question or statement when trying to explain something to them, or give instructions on how to take medications, or take care of their problem. They aren't being rude but they aren't concentrating on what could be a very important part of their visit. No wonder they don't get better. You, the patient, need to be a part of the decision making and the treatment plan.

When your doctor is examining you, it is important not to talk unless to answer a question and certainly not while he or she is taking your blood pressure or listening to your heart or lungs with a stethoscope.

None of us will live forever and although we may not like to think or talk about it, it is very appropriate to do so and well before that day comes. And you need to do this with your doctor after you have completed an Advanced Directive (Living Will or Durable Power of Attorney), or designated someone, preferably in writing, as your proxy to make end of life decisions for you should you become incapacitated.

You can change your mind anytime on what you put in your Advanced Directive but to wait until you are near death some day makes it difficult to arrive at meaningful decisions that will make it easier on you and your family as well as your doctor, who, unless otherwise directed by you, tends to perform heroic measures. You need to know your options, ranging from doing everything heroic to maintaining life, to just comfort care. The Terri Schiavo dilemma brought all this out in a terribly agonizing way.

Discussing what you've put in your Advanced Directive with your doctor should give you some reassurance that he or she will try to carry you and your family through this difficult time. Then you leave a copy with your doctor and give copies to each of your children after discussing it with each of them, making sure they all agree. And have one available to take with you to the hospital should you become acutely ill, or even if you are going in to the hospital for an elective surgical procedure. And travel with a copy and put the current copy in your journal (see Write-Therapy below). Age 18 is the right time to write your initial Advanced Directive.

Keep your health records, including a copy of your Advanced Directive, in a manila folder or preferably a note book (or a computer, if you wish, but this isn't very 'private'). Ask your doctor for a copy of your laboratory tests, x-ray and pathology reports and file them chronologically. If you see a physician in consultation who sends a report to your doctor, ask for a copy. If you fill out forms detailing your past history, family history, current problems, etc., make a copy and file this as well. Record the details of the health problems of blood relatives. This may someday be very important when genetics becomes a part of every day medical practice.

You are responsible for your health, in partnership with your doctor. It is the privilege of the physician to help you in every way we can, but we can't do it without you!

♦ **Your patients will respond depending on how much they respect you!**

There are several situations that deal with the patient-physician encounter that warrant a little extra attention here:

The difficult patient. I define the difficult patient as not the psychotic person or someone with a severe personality disorder but someone who is angry at
1) a colleague(s)/partner(s) of yours
2) another physician(s)
3) you
4) the health care system
5) life
6) themselves
7) all of the above

And now you are asked to see them by the receptionist, the chair of your division or department, a patient-'friend', or you don't realize that they are a 'difficult patient' until you encounter them in your office. They can be angry for many reasons but maybe the most common one is the arrogance they have encountered within the medical system; and now they want to sue someone. Somebody has to see these people; or, you can do to them what a number of physicians before you may have done—refuse to see them or shuttle them to someone else.

But they deserve a hearing (in the true sense of the word) as these people are 1) the most likely to sue, 2) the least compliant, 3) very expensive to the health care system, and 4) the ones most likely to seek alternatives to the traditional system of medicine (this includes alternative/complementary as well as quackery medicine), and it is easy to say, "Let them go," but as I said they deserve a hearing. They may truly have a significant disease as well as a legitimate gripe.

It is estimated that about 15% of patients would be classified as 'difficult'. These patients are more likely to have a mental disorder, many somatic complaints, more severe symptoms, more unmet expectations and higher use of health care services. A significant statistic is that physicians with... 'poorer psychosocial attitudes' experience 3 fold more encounters with what would be considered difficult patients (23% versus 8%).

In my over 35 years of practicing medicine I saw a lot of these people and I think over 90% can be appeased and brought back into the mainstream; but it may take a few visits as well as the desire to do so.

There are a few rules to follow and are for the most part a reiteration of what I have already said earlier:

- Begin by telling him or her how much time you have for this visit and reschedule accordingly, if necessary.
- If the encounter is in the hospital setting, be sure you have complete privacy.
- Communicate, and this means LISTEN. You have got to let them talk out why they are angry, and sometimes, this may be all that it takes. Use their name regularly. You are letting them have some control which they feel they have lost, along with their dignity. Try to establish a partnership by using "we" instead of "I" or "you", when appropriate.
- While listening, you maintain eye contact and appropriate head nods and frowns as you empathize with them. You further empathize by saying, "I'm sorry you are so angry and unhappy," or, "I appreciate your anger and imagine that it is making you miserable." Caution on apologizing too soon for the physician or the system they are angry with, as it may not be their fault, but there is a good chance they are. However, until you know all the facts, withhold judgment as the patient may be litigious and quote to others everything you say. On the other hand, proper and carefully handling of this patient may avoid litigation. This takes some diplomacy and control on your part as will as the careful practice of the Art of Medicine. Yet, you need to let the patient know you will help him or her work through this, if possible.

- ♦ **Empathy turns defensiveness around. Defensiveness is a paradox of the human condition: our survival and security seem to depend on self-assertion and defense, but intimacy and cooperation require that we risk being vulnerable!** (MP Nichols).

- Body language is extremely important in dealing with the difficult patient. While looking them in the eye, sit at or below their eye level, at least at the initial visit, and lean forward towards them every now and then. This again gives them a little sense of control and autonomy.
- Don't let your anger at why you have to see them show. Be calm. Keep the tone of your voice calm. They would like to get in an argument with you, to really vent their anger, but then, they've won and you've lost, and they go on to the next physician.
- Try to find a way to agree with them on something, that they are 'right'.
- Smile accordingly. You are trying to establish rapport which you have to do before there can be mutual trust.
- Use appropriate but cautious 'touch therapy'. Shake hands at the beginning and the end of your visit. Pat them on the back on the way out of the office while complimenting them on managing a difficult situation: "I know that this has been tough on you."
- Ultimately, you will need to pin the patient down as to why they specifically are angry, as they may have rambled on in trying to get their side of the story out. You must find out what their unmet expectations are; they may be unrealistic but the previous physician(s) never dealt with them. Prior to

your next visit with the patient ask them to write out their expectations in the order of their importance and which ones weren't met. (Unmet expectations are a significant contributor to patient dissatisfaction. You might inquire into these before the patient becomes a 'difficult patient' if you sense an element of dissatisfaction.) This isn't always easy to sort out because you may only have their side of the story. At this point you tell them you need to find out more about the situation and see them again. Then you can ask what they would like you to offer to help. Be sure each of you has a plan.

The patient wants to feel that it makes a big difference
To the physician whether they want to improve
The patient's well-being, and
Whether they live or die!

- Ask about the patient's emotions, their feelings. Note that anger can be a front for fear.
- Studies show that the incidence of depression in these people is about twice that of the population. Maybe, if a physician had dealt with this earlier the problem you're seeing them for wouldn't be there. Eventually you'll need to deal with the possibility of a depression, but I don't recommend doing this at the first visit, unless the patient brings it up. In fact, it may take several visits and the establishment of some trust before you can attempt to unmask this. *Every depressed patient is angry!* But not every angry patient is depressed.
- Carefully record the results of the interview into the record.

A word about the 'difficult family member' is appropriate here. Usually this is a spouse but it could be a child or a sibling of the patient, or even a parent, who, up to this point has been fairly reasonable to deal with. That is, until this family member decides to take their anger out on the physician and the medical system, even though there may not be a basis for it with this particular patient-physician relationship. At this point, the patient has to realize that his or her relative is jeopardizing his care, and probably not with just this physician.

If you can appease the 'difficult patient' as I have described them, you can be very proud of yourself—you are practicing the Art of Medicine.

Managing the violent or potentially violent patient is another matter and you won't likely know this until you encounter them or the police ask you to intervene with the unarmed patient. Don't ignore the patient or their threats. Be vigilant and closely observe their body language while encouraging them to talk. Listen to their concerns and questions. Don't allow a lull in the conversation to occur. Your body language must be calm and reassuring that you are interested in helping, but keep your distance from them—don't encroach on their personal space. And never turn your back to them or let them get between you and the door. Document everything that went on in the medical record. Get help.

Covering for another physician. No physician can work 7 days a week for long periods. The public knows this. The hospitalized patient being covered by a physician that is new to their problem is disconcerting to the patient—it is perceived as being disruptive to the continuity of care they expect. The physician going off the service, even for the weekend, needs to discuss or leave written instructions to the covering physician, and this physician needs to let the patient know he or she is aware of all the pertinent facts. In this situation, I would ask the covering physician, "How would you want your family cared for in this situation?"—the Platinum Rule of Medicine again.

The cancer patient in remission. Maybe your patient has been in remission many years to the point the physician almost forgets about it or is no longer concerned about it. But the patient is concerned. They still need to discuss their feelings about the cancer with the physician every now and then. And the physician should let the patient know he or she is always ready to discuss the concerns the patient has—you are there for them.

Compliment them on how they have so bravely handled it. Encourage involvement in a support group or to resume going if they used to go to one. As time goes on, there will be more and more cancer survivors, but this doesn't lessen the individual support the patient needs from you.

Avoiding a malpractice suit. A young physician just going into practice entertains an appreciable risk of being involved in a malpractice lawsuit during the course of a lifetime of practice. The best way of not being sued is to reduce your risks.

Lichtstein et al have summarized this nicely in a number of articles, pointing out that in more than 80% of suits, communication and interpersonal factors accounted for the precipitating cause of an unhappy patient bringing suit. It is known that only ~5% of patients who might have a legitimate reason for a suit, do so. And most of those who do sue don't have a true basis for a suit. They're just angry for the impersonal care they were given, usually in an arrogant manner.

The most common allegations of negligence are misdiagnosis, improper treatment or improperly performed procedure, and improper administration of medication. One of the most common claims of an improperly performed procedure is the physical exam— something serious was missed.

The following is a reminder list of risk factors for a lawsuit. I've already mentioned almost all of these but it is so important to your future as well as the quality of care you deliver to your patients, they are worth mentioning again. *Quality is what the patient/customer thinks it is!*

1) Communicate with the patient, and the family if needed. This includes listening effectively.
2) If a mistake has been made, admit it right away and give them all the facts. Record this in the history. Make decisions quickly on what to do next.
3) Say "I'm sorry" when appropriate and necessary, including if a mistake has been made. Not saying it when appropriate is arrogance to the patient.
4) Avoid arrogance. Arrogance will eventually get you in trouble and may be the only reason the patient is suing. Always tell the patient if you are not making rounds this weekend, or going off the service, or will be away when they are scheduled to return for their next visit. If possible, introduce them to the doctor who will be covering or replacing you, and certainly give them his or her name.
5) Establish mutual trust with the patient.

6) Be accessible. This includes returning phone calls promptly.
7) Provide continuity of care. Shuttling the patient around to different doctors produces a sense of abandonment.
8) Spend time with the patient.
9) Contact the patient with an abnormal test result as soon as the results are available. This stresses the importance of a tickler file.
10) Get 2nd opinions. Make the call, write the letter. Know when you don't know.
11) Document. Document. Document. If you don't document, it didn't happen. Never alter the record.
12) Caution on what you put in writing.

Everything that can be invented has been invented!
(steam engine, electricity and the telegraph)
[Charles Duell, US Patent Office Commissioner,
urging President McKinley to abolish the office—1899]

13) Control your anger, no matter how upset you might be with the patient.
14) Never speak or write disparagingly of another physician.
15) If the patient doesn't follow through with your advice, put it in the record.
16) Do not abandon or desert the patient, or even perceive to do so.
17) Practice the Platinum Rule of Medicine.

If you think some of these things take too much of your time, wait until you see the time involved to be named in a malpractice suit!

There is nothing that can prepare you for how to cope with a medical malpractice lawsuit, but I suggest reading Sara Charles' many articles on this. She points out that over 95% of physicians develop some form of emotional disorder as a result of being named, even when it clearly isn't your fault. Recall my comments above that the majority of suits brought aren't because of true malpractice, but more out of anger. Your integrity has been challenged and you are sure your name will be headlines in your local newspaper; surprisingly, this rarely happens. Most sued physicians are eventually vindicated! Remember this. The challenge against you is not so much your competence but your pocketbook.

In the meantime, deal with it head on. Talk to your lawyer, get your options. The lawyer will probably tell you that you aren't to talk to anyone about it but you must. You can't live with this alone. There may even be support groups of previously sued physicians in your community to help you. If you haven't already done so, make a list of all your professional educational activities, the lectures you have attended. Update your curriculum vitae, but don't enhance it; that could really get you in trouble.

Deal with stress factors as I have listed in the section on Stress and Burnout. Take vacations and do your best not to think about the suit, put it out of your mind. Talk to yourself. Someday, it will be behind you. Exercise. Read for leisure. Be kind to yourself and *Forgive yourself!* It's easy for me to say, but practice all the 'don't worry' comments I have in this book. A hundred years from now, this won't mean a thing (actually, it will be much, much sooner than that but the hundred-year milestone puts it all in context). Remember, you will be remembered for what you do for others, for the hundreds, probably thousands of patients you have helped, not this one event.

Finally, write-it-out. I've mentioned this before but the value of Write-Therapy in this situation may be significant (see below). Write out everything you want to about your involvement with the suit. Then throw it away, possibly sharing it with a trusted colleague first. You can re-write it as often as you want. It's a catharsis. It probably puts the whole thing in a niche in your cortex rather than on the front burner.

This, too, shall pass!

The interactions among physicians has changed appreciably in my over 45 years in the practice of medicine. There is less collegiality, less interchange of ideas, more a sense of competition. From my discussions with physicians around the country, I don't see these changes nearly as great at Mayo as elsewhere but I'm concerned about this. In the first half of my career, we almost always had time each day to share a cup of coffee with 1, or more often, several colleagues, and not always with just those from my division. We had 2 or 3 evening education-oriented dinner meetings a month. And I knew almost every staff physician at Mayo when we had nearly 500 physicians and PhD scientists.

The collegial coffee breaks rarely happen any more—we're too busy. If you take an extra 15 minutes for a coffee break, you get home 15 minutes later. Two career families and busy evening activities of the children have impacted on evenings out—you soon get out of the habit of going to some of these meetings. But these gatherings offered a chance for a bonding with a lot of your colleagues versus a bonding with just a few on the tennis court or golf course. As I have said several times already, this social interaction is extremely important for stress reduction. It might be the only time a stressed physician can unburden himself to someone whom he is comfortable with but not otherwise seek out for help and advice.

In academic medical centers it seems that we are consumed with committee activities and meetings, non educational meetings. Committees in any setting diffuse responsibility to the point that firm decisions become difficult.

♦ **Meetings: None of us is as dumb as all of us!**

Through these encounters there is frequently an exchange of ideas that might lead to better treatment of a patient's problem, or to a paper for publication. There is another positive aspect to collegiality and that is an opportunity to discuss interesting 'great cases' with one or more colleagues, especially if you came up with the diagnosis and/or successful treatment. This is ego boosting and one of the fun aspects of medicine; we all need this now and then. You can only get this kind of boost from another physician.

♦ **Collegiality is a shared goal of common purpose while according respect for each other!** (Jay Jayasanker)

Our profession seems to be unique in requiring some collegiality to promote its professionalism in our singular goal of promoting the health of society, as advocates of the patient. Lawyers are in much greater competition with each other than we are, but we are becoming more competitive as we go from covenant to contract, *from profession to occupation*. We have lost much of the cooperative spirit, which is one of the necessities to professionalism. We are becoming disconnected from each other and this isn't good for our profession.

I don't have any good ideas on how to restore collegiality to our lives. If all of us attended one more evening education meetings per year, it might begin to add up. Join a service organization or arrange a 'social' lunch once a month with some of your colleagues. If you have the right chemistry of attendees, pretty soon you will begin to look forward to the next lunch weeks ahead. But be careful that not just bitch sessions.

Next to your children the influence you can have on the lives of young medical students, residents and fellows and nurses is tremendous and rewarding. We owe it to the profession and the public to do this right. I include nurses because I think we need to take a greater role in teaching them, nurturing their careers and encouraging them. Take student nurses on rounds with you or into the patient's room in the outpatient setting. Explain to the patient who they are and ask if OK to do this.

There are common sense ways to deal with medical students and residents. After all, didn't many of us elect to be in academia? And without medical students and residents there would be no academia, or a future of the profession!

Don't get so sidetracked with administration and research and committees that the students become your lowest priority. Teaching can be one of the most rewarding things you do. Later, when you encounter them they will excitedly recall the role you played in their education and maturity. Their response to you will tend to be how much they respect you.

First of all, remember when you were a student? You can probably vividly recall the residents and attendings who were nice to you, or demeaning to you. Those in between may blur a little. If you have interaction with them, even if only to give a lecture, you are one of their role models. Are you the role model you would want your children to encounter if they were in medicine?

I have repeatedly stressed the value of being a role model to all those around you. This is character building and becomes a form of self-continuous improvement. In the mid 80's JAMA published a letter in the A Piece of My Mind section from a very disgruntled young physician who just completed a residency in a major medical center. The physician made the following statements: *We work like slaves, get very little sleep, have no formal didactic teaching. We just get degrading letters in our mailboxes about how poorly we have performed. They've 'taught' me to feel afraid, worthless, ashamed....they have dehumanized us. It is sad that people so bright and so famous have lost the ability to do a simple thing—to treat all people as equals.*

No matter what the emotional state of this writer was, JAMA did publish the A Piece of My Mind letter along with the name of the major medical center! And the writer's name! I have since heard of a medical student from this center saying he found no role models in his 4 years of school to pattern himself after. Probably many students and residents in most medical centers have had the bad luck to draw a fair number of attendings and teachers who did not respect them. We have to ask ourselves, "Am I treating younger physicians with respect?" *Would I want my daughter or son to be treated the way I treat young physicians in training?* "Or young physicians newly in practice?" I don't think so. To rationalize that this was the way we were treated is no excuse. These physicians with a bitter experience will likely become negative role models. We must break this cycle of abuse.

♦ **The secret of education is respecting the pupil!** (Ralph Waldo Emerson)

On hospital rounds or seeing patients together in the outpatient areas, you are allowing them to learn the art of medicine from you—there is no other way to 'teach' it. They'll be watching your interaction with the family and the health care personnel as well.

Always be kind and patient with them, never threatening. Give them time to think through an answer to your question. Be accepting of an "I don't know" from them.

Teach physical diagnosis every chance you get. This is truly another lost art in medicine. Every so often observe them doing a complete history and physical examination on a patient.

Don't forget that you may have years of experience on them and can intuitively assess the severity of a patient's illness in minutes, that might take them hours or even days.

Stimulate them with questions and always compliment them when appropriate. If you have criticism of their performance, give it to them in private and make it constructive; find something positive to add. Don't wait until the end of the rotation and just put the criticisms in their record without discussing it with them first—that is why you are there. As I mentioned above, many physicians have children, nieces, nephews and family friends in medical training. Wouldn't you want them nurtured, honed, molded, shaped by a true role model that cares?

How do the students and residents interpret your body language? Your attitude? Be attuned to their stress and possible personal problems they might be having. Are they depressed? You must be sensitive to this, and act on it accordingly. The other students and residents will pick up on this first, and they may come to you to deal with this. You will need to console them when they make a mistake, or their patient dies; and they will make mistakes. They are vulnerable and sometimes overly sensitive. Deal with it today. *They will never forget you for it.* I can promise you that.

The bottom line is *respect* them. Someday, one or more of them may be taking care of your patients, as well as your family, and even more scary, *you!*

Until recently **mentoring** of young physicians has been informal only, a happenstance of two compatible people who have very mutual interests. The physician in this case is kind of a temporary advisor who derives personal satisfaction from seeing others succeed. Now, most teaching hospitals are formalizing the program of mentorship, especially for young faculty. Keep in mind what I said earlier that mentoring was one of the two most important assets (the other was time management) for the successful college student; so mentoring is critical to all young people, not just medical students and residents.

Mentoring isn't easy; senior as well as junior staff members are usually not interested for different reasons. Foremost, the physician has to want to be a mentor. Second, he or she must be given some time to do this, and third, he or she needs to be rewarded.

There are specific characteristics to being a mentor and a mentor is different than a role model. All (good) mentors are probably positive role models but most role models are not mentors. A mentor is almost always older than the mentee but a role model can be any age. Role models are not necessarily interactive with the person learning from them. This is sometimes referred to as 'elbow knowledge'.

> ♦ **Some people climbing the ladder of success find that when they get near the top that the ladder is leaning against the wrong wall!**

A good mentor-mentee relationship should help avoid this.

The mentee should select the mentor after due process of establishing that the mentor has mutual interests and goals and is 'compatible' with the mentee, as a good mentorship can last for years. The mentor also must "screen" the potential mentee. A

127

productive mentorship involves mutual trust. Some physicians are much better mentors than others and may be in demand for this responsibility. In fairness to the young physician, he or she may have to say "no", but could guide the mentee to equally as effective mentors.

Bhagia and Tinsley have nicely summarized the mentoring partnership. They point out that the relationship must remain professional rather than purely personal, but this doesn't mean that the two can't be good friends. However, the mentor shouldn't have to shoulder the personal problems of the mentee; this can destroy an otherwise effective mentorship.

Rewarding the mentor in the academic setting is important, namely through academic promotion. Putting the names of the mentees (per pre-established set of guidelines for mentorship) in their CV could be similar to listing post-doc fellows as researchers do.

The following are guidelines for an effective mentorship:

The Mentor—Mentee Relationship
- Each mutually agreeable that goals are similar and can work together
- Mutual respect
- Obligation to put each other's names on a paper depends on each's contributions
- Don't expect an effective mentorship to occur via e-mail

The Mentor
- Supportive. Assists in setting goals and evaluates progress
- Someone of high integrity
- Respectful of the mentee. Friendly
- Available
- Non self-serving; doesn't use the mentee to promote his own goals
- Honest. Gives constructive feedback
- Helps network
- Promotes professional growth
- Helps with CV and academic promotion
- Involves the mentee in national societies
- Is a role model
- Guides them into a balanced lifestyle; teaches time management skills
- Asks stimulating and challenging questions
- Resourceful
- Nurtures their own mentoring skills
- Knows when the mentorship should end

I like to tell young physicians going into practice or academia that the pace of accomplishments always comes slower than wished for or expected. This is normal. They are like the bamboo tree:

The bamboo tree
As a seedling, it spends its first 4 years spreading its roots.
In its 5th year it grows 40 feet!

In summary, a mentor nurtures a young professional into the best possible person he or she can be.

The Mentee
- Is clear in his goals and how the mentor fits in to these
- Has no unreasonable expectations
- Respectful of the mentor's time commitment
- Keeps it professional
- Appreciative of the mentor's contributions but doesn't feel obligated to repay in any way
- Knows when the mentorship should end

A true mentor doesn't expect any kind of payback, but the mentee can honor his mentor by 1) acquiring and exhibiting some of the positive character traits of the mentor and role model, and 2) someday becoming a mentor himself. The mentor leaves a personal and professional legacy(s) that will be remembered long after he or she is gone. It is truly a commitment to the lives of others. The mentor is a better professional because of the time he or she took to nurture someone else.

♦ **Mentoring relieves the grieving over my own mortality!**

Relating well to the **referring physician** is imperative; not doing so is perceived as arrogance. Find a way to compliment him or her to the patient and to the physician directly. Keep him informed of what is going on with regular phone calls (emails are OK if material not sensitive) and caution on relegating this to the house staff. If you are a specialist, the referring physician may be of the same specialty and didn't refer the patient to you to only be seen by a resident. A summary letter should go out within 3 working days of dismissing the patient from your care, but offer to remain involved.

I have some strong feelings about the importance of the relationships between referring and referred physicians. There is an increasing disinterest in referring patients for another expert opinion, mostly because it will come out of his or her overhead as dictated by the HMO, or a 3rd party payer who won't authorize it (sometimes the 'authority' is just a high school graduate). Seeking another opinion for your patient is the heart of professionalism—doing what is best for the patient! This should be a part of the patient's bill of rights.

The patients as a group must become more vocally outspoken on their as well as their physicians' right and obligation to get other opinions. These opinions also serve as a form of education for the physicians—we can always learn from each other, unless, of course, the physician knows everything! If he knew everything, then why isn't his patient getting better!

A second or even a third opinion can bring peace of mind to the patient as well as the physician that the right course of action is being taken. There is an unwritten etiquette or protocol in the interaction between the referring and the referred physicians.

The referring physician should

- Select the best physician he or she knows of that is capable of assessing the problem.
- Call the referred physician if there are intricacies to the problem that may not be in the written report. Otherwise, a letter along with appropriate laboratory and imaging studies must accompany the patient.

- Let the referred physician, and the patient, know exactly why he or she is seeing the patient.

The referred physician should

- See the patient within a reasonable period of time.
- Call the referring physician the day you see the patient, and if not available, leave a voice message or e-mail him if there is no confidential information involved.
- Keep the physician informed of the progress such as after an endoscopic procedure or imaging study, and of course, before and after a surgical procedure.
- Find a way to compliment the physician including to his patient. I said this before but I'm saying it again because it enhances trust in the health care system.
- The frequency of the communication depends on the 'urgency' of the problem such that a letter sent out within 3 working days may be sufficient in most cases.
- Always return the patient to the referring physician. Sometimes the patient asks if you'll assume their primary care, at least of their 'organ-specific' problem. This can be a touchy situation and needs to be resolved by the three parties involved. The best way might be for the patient to ask his or her physician to be able to continue to see the referred physician at intervals, assuming the referred physician agrees.
- An academic center's future clinical reputation can depend on how the physicians deal with the referring physician. The staff shouldn't delegate the communication responsibility to a first year resident, or maybe any resident.
- I don't like the term "LMD" (Local Medical Doctor), as in some centers it has a negative connotation, a physician of 'inferior' knowledge. To these physicians using the term LMD, I suggest going and work in the 'trenches' with an 'LMD' and see what it is like out there.
- I think it is very important that academic centers assume an obligation to go out into the referring communities to lecture and to put on 1 or 2 day update courses in the academic center at regular intervals, at little charge to the attending physician.
- One major pet peeve of referring subspecialists is to have their patient taken care of by 'only' a subspecialty fellow who knows less about the subspecialty than the referring physician. The attending staff must keep this in mind.

Gender to gender: Since the late 90's, female physicians have accounted for over half the physicians graduating from medical schools. When I was the Internal Medicine Residency Program Director at Mayo in the 80's with over 150 residents at any one time, I recognized the calming effect the women physicians brought to the program in addition to being compassionate caring physicians. The patients brought out their maternal instincts.

But the literature and anecdotal experience says women physicians aren't always treated equally, including by patients and nurses. A woman physician as a part of the team might not be asked to go to lunch 'with the boys', or asked her opinion, or given due recognition for academic promotion, or leadership roles. I've seen significant progress in all these areas, but I urge that we remind ourselves the tremendous value women physicians bring to the practice of the Art of Medicine.

- **In the days of the giants, a giant rarely left work early to pick up a sick child at day care!**

We all make **mistakes**, it is human nature. In the medical profession, these can have fatal consequences. Yet, there is rarely ever anyone to talk to about them among ourselves, let alone to someone outside the medical profession. And certainly not at a conference in front of our peers. It would seem to be an admission of a sin, a realization that we're not perfect!

If the medical profession can't accept that their members make mistakes, then neither can society. Nothing in our training teaches us how to handle mistakes. In academic centers where a whole hierarchy of physicians might be involved in the care of a patient, it is easy to spread the blame around, diffusing the guilt. Most physicians 'learn to live with their mistakes'.

We isolate ourselves from healing, further aggravating the stress we are under and maybe even precipitating a lurking depression. This could bring about making more mistakes as well as practicing more 'defensive medicine' by ordering unnecessary but expensive and risky tests.

Men especially find it difficult to admit they made a mistake, instead, carrying around tremendous emotional baggage their wives don't begin to understand.

The best way to handle this is to be up front and honest with the patient and the family right away, giving them facts about the situation and answering all questions. Patients want this and are coming to expect it. This takes some maturity on the part of the physician, and, as we would tell our children, it is 'character building'. And record the results of your discussion in the patient's record.

Whether this confession is enough for the physician's peace of mind depends on many things. Ideally, if the physician can discuss this with 1 or 2 colleagues including a mentor, this would help tremendously. As I discussed in the section on dealing with medical malpractice lawsuits, practice Write-Therapy. At a minimum in the quiet alone, write out what happened, your role in it, what you would do differently and what you learned from it. Take 20 minutes to an hour to do this. Before destroying the paper, consider sharing this with a trusted colleague while in his or her presence if you are reluctant to talk about it. Then destroy the paper. Repeat this writing exercise if necessary. Interestingly, studies show that this exercise is effective in initiating the forgetting process. Why, is poorly understood but is probably a form of closure. You need to go on with your life. To personally carry this burden, maybe for years, is unfair to you, your family, your partners, and your patients. You will ultimately be better for it once you deal with it. We have and will all make mistakes! *To err is human.* It's a part of life.

The definition of the **impaired physician** and other health professionals is almost certainly the same in every state but the manner of reporting one and the handling can vary from state to state. The regulating agency and the statutes are governed by the state legislatures and all the regulations are listed on their web sites.

The impaired health professional is someone unable to practice their profession with reasonable skill and safety by reason of illness, use of alcohol, drugs, or chemicals. Or as a result of any mental, physical or psychological condition. Sexual misconduct and other acts that result in a serious risk of harm to the public or to themselves also come under the purview of the regulating agency.

By law a physician aware of the misconduct of a health professional listed above must report it to the regulating agency. I suggest keeping detailed confidential notes regarding this individual, including dates, and sign your note. Others witnessing this misconduct should do the same or countersign the note(s). You are immune from civil liability or criminal prosecution for submitting a report in good faith. These reports are confidential and privileged communication.

Finally, in regard to you as a physician, never burn your bridges. It is so easy in a moment of anger or frustration to tell someone off, or worse, put it in writing. I have seen this many times, only to come back and haunt the person, maybe even to the point of keeping the physician from a promotion, or returning to the institution after quitting and finding the grass wasn't really greener than it was supposed to be.

I have previously discussed **your health**, which involves a relationship with one or more physicians, but it is worth repeating some of these tenets because your life may depend on it! Have your own primary care physician but do not manage your own workup or self medicate. Get an exam every 1 to 3 years, according to your age and risk factors—this is imperative. You owe it to your family, as well as yourself. Self-care is now one of the tenets of professionalism. When asked to take care of another physician or his or her family, be sure of the expectations and of maintaining confidentiality. I know of physicians suing other physicians!

You have an obligation to keep up in the science of medicine—you should NEVER stop learning or wanting to learn. This is one of the principles of a professional. You probably gain the most in educating your peers; don't shun the opportunity to do this.

**Learning is not compulsory,
but neither is survival!**

Edward Denning

YOUR RELATIONSHIP TO PEOPLE YOU WORK WITH

This subject may seem out of place in a discussion of the Art of Medicine but a dysfunctional work place ultimately affects the care of the patient, and the work ethic of the employees in <u>any</u> business. And you, the physician, may not see a role here for yourself but there is. Because your associates may not be as caring about these people is all the more reason you must be involved. At this time you may have no aspirations for leadership but that could change in time. Or, you head up some hospital or HMO committees, or become responsible for recruiting physicians to your group.

♦ **If all health care administrators were laid end to end......**
....it would probably be a good thing!

At a minimum, you relate to nurses and office personnel on a daily basis, as well as other physicians. If you are in academia, you will almost certainly be involved with a lot of committee work involving a number of ancillary health care personnel.

The difference between mediocrity and greatness is the
Feeling you have for one another!
Vince Lombardi
NFL coach

We're talking about mutual respect here and we don't need to define it—you know what this is. It's the Golden Rule!

If you can't relate well to the people you work with or who work for you, to show each and every one mutual respect, then you're probably not doing very well with your patients. Study after study show that employees, including nurses, leave their job, not so much because of salary and benefits, but because they don't feel appreciated or don't feel they are considered a part of the team. In one study two-thirds report never receiving praise or recognition for good work done.

The deepest principle in human nature is the
Craving to be appreciated!
William James

And to be loved. This is recognizing the person, any person you work with, for what they do, and that their work is important to others. This kind of interaction shouldn't be assigned to someone, or a committee; it is the responsibility of everyone, but especially the physicians. It should be a part of the culture you work in and contribute to. If you look for the good in everyone and treat every person with dignity and respect, you'll have very few problems. *Work lets us feel needed.*

If you have the ability to make people feel valued and
Important in your presence,
You have met the number one human need!

This is your character coming through in the form of gentleness and humility, a humility of strength and self control. You care!

I can live a month on a good compliment
Mark Twain

Actually, studies show a good compliment remains in the front burner of the memory for only about 2 weeks but an inappropriate criticism can be remembered for months, and resurrected in the mind every time the perpetrator is seen or mentioned. Non constructive criticism will destroy almost every incentive to improve.

♦ **Never underestimate the value of a compliment!**

Over 100% of people appreciate a genuine compliment! Recognition is about thanking people, listening to them and treating them with dignity and respect. Nearly 20% of patients say they are turned off by rudeness of the physician's receptionist and other personnel, some to the point of going elsewhere. Someone (you?) need to deal with this head on. The health care worker must be reminded at regular intervals to never discuss patient's confidential data with someone not concerned with the patient's care and to look in the file for only data they need to know about. Other than nurses or physician's assistants, office personnel have no reason to read the physician's notes unless they are taking transcription or coding.

♦ **If you take good care of your employees, they will take good care of your customers!**

Job efficiency and attitude declines significantly if people are forced to work with rude or bullying personnel in any employment. You, the physician, can't tolerate this in any of the people you work with. They pass this attitude on to the patients. Almost all employees are more productive when around positive people, and are more likely to stay with the organization.

♦ **Be as nice to the custodian as you are to the top guy!**

In regards to the RN-physician relationship, this deserves even more attention; there is definitely an opportunity for improvement here! We are in a crisis mode in this country from a nursing shortage and it is going to get worse before it gets better. We must do everything we can to improve the working relationships we have with nurses, as well as physician-assistants and nurse practitioners. They are part of the team, the family we work with, with a goal of helping our patients. Can you imagine your job without nurses? But there are many anecdotal stories of nurses quitting the profession, not just their job, but their profession because of the lack of respect from physicians.

Remember, in the hospital the nurses not uncommonly spend up to 12 hours with one of your sick patients. They are skilled personnel. They greatly influence the outcome of the patient's hospital stay. And many stay beyond their working hours because of their compassion. When one of your and their patients die, they grieve, too. And they were probably with the patient when they died. We need to learn how to deal with their grief—it's real.

I advocate that every group of physicians, whether private practice or academic medicine, that relates to the nurses discuss on a regular basis at their practice committee meetings how to improve their rapport with the nurses, and then do something about it. Make an open invitation to the nurses to accompany you (and the team if in academic medicine) on rounds and ask their opinion about various situations. Invite them and include them in your teaching conferences. Include them in your social activities. Have a special nurses' day in your hospital during national nurses' recognition week. Several times a year, bring in special goodies to the nursing station for everyone. Celebrate the profession of caring. Always celebrate National Nurses Day.

Take special interest in the student nurses. Nurture them. Invite them on rounds and to your conferences. Encourage them to ask you questions. They are your future employees, but only if you respect them. Leadership needs to deal with those physicians who demonstrate lack of mutual respect to anyone, not just the nurses.

Nurses have great public trust and respect—we must recognize and appreciate this. The following quote should be posted on the wall at every nursing station.

The trained nurse has been one of the greatest blessings of humanity,
Taking a place beside the physician, the priest, and
Inferior to neither in her mission!
Sir William Osler

Go out of your way to compliment and thank the nurses that take care of your patients.

A form letter to dozens or thousands of employees is not nearly as effective as the personal touch. Lee Iacocca frequented the assembly lines of Chrysler, talking to the workers and praising them, with results that made history. A positive handwritten note from you can mean more to some people than a bonus. Put a copy in their file. If you really want to tell them how much they are appreciated, write a note to their spouse and family. They will never forget this. This makes the employee feel as a part of the team, and appreciated!

And remember, call them or greet them by name, not just "Hi", or just "Good morning." And smile! This is easier if you come to work with a smile. And a positive attitude!

Learn the names of the people you encounter but don't work closely with like the custodians or the hospital volunteers. They are all part of your work family.

- ◆ **R.A. is known for his ability to communicate with employees at every level!** (is CEO of company with >20,000 employees)

- ◆ **We wildly underestimate the power of the tiniest personal touch!** (Tom Peters)

Control your temper, in fact *never* get angry. *You can measure the size of a person by what makes him or her angry!* Never cast blame.

- ◆ **A great man shows his greatness by the way he treats the little man!** (Caryle)

- ◆ **Be nice to the people on your way up the ladder—you'll meet them again on your way back down!**

When I am angry at myself, I criticize others!
Ed Howe

- ◆ **Never argue with a fool who has nothing to lose!**

Teamwork is what you are striving for. It is the fuel that allows common people to attain uncommon results. The good employees need to be given increased responsibilities and the courage to fail, providing they learn from it and move on. It creates a resilience that is important to growth. The employee should be encouraged to think and be rewarded and recognized for going the extra mile and creating innovations that improve on the efficiency and ambiance of the work place. They can't do this if they encounter arrogance, rudeness, or abuse from their superiors and no respect. These are fairly common in the work place, even in health care work places. Besides lack of efficiency this atmosphere creates a significant amount of stress.

♦   **Only dead fish swim with the stream!**

When employees begin to deal with customers (patients) as an imposition on their time, or leaders who rely on structures and/or only the bottom line rather than people, you know you are in trouble.

Mutual trust and *respect* is essential in the work place. The leaders need to celebrate with those they are working with. *Attitude is the number one quality to look for in recruiting personnel.* You must never allow an employee with a positive attitude to lose this.

Consider *mutual respect rounds*; every 6 or 8 weeks at one of the clinical practice meetings where you discuss practice issues, discuss issues related to lack of mutual respect including anonymously reported negative comments about a physician in your group from patients and employees. No names are mentioned. This may take less than 5 minutes of the meeting time, with the goal of having none to discuss! Hearing these comments usually incites some self-reflection. It's also appropriate at this time to relay nice, positive comments. Record these.

I would like to see where all medical centers incorporate quarterly into their grand rounds or department education conference the principles of the Art of Medicine. This would include some of the tenets of the core competencies I've discussed earlier. Nurses and other health care personnel would be invited and involved, including being responsible for at least one of these a year. It is imperative that the leadership be present at all of these.

You can make the difference between a happy, loyal, effective long-term employee, or one who's embittered and a negative influence on all those around them. You are the role model to all the people you work with. You should be open to mentoring some of these people.

♦   **They may forget what you said, but they will never forget how you made them feel!**

Recognition is a cure for many ills!
John Nash
("Brilliant Mind")

Service in the Medical 'Industry'

When we think of service we think of our interactions with clerks at retail stores, including their employers and the inherent trust we have in the products they sell. But the medical 'industry' may be the epitome in service, at least Len Berry thinks so. He is a guru in marketing service in the business world and has written extensively on it with the best summary of the value of service in his book *Discovering the Soul of Service*. We don't like to think of our patients as 'customers' but that is what has come about for the many reasons I've discussed in this book.

People don't buy a Cadillac because they think GM needs the money!

Service includes the delivery of health care beyond that of the technical/scientific aspects of diagnostic and therapeutic procedures. The vast majority of the public thinks there is a crisis in their health care delivery and it isn't just the costs—a lot of it is the lack of good service which can include timely access, and the ability to see the same doctor at each visit, especially a doctor who truly cares about them. Remember, *quality is what the customer thinks it is*.

In health care the physician is the primary deliverer of service and his or her service delivery not only likely affects the outcome of the patient's health, but the health care employees will use the physician as a role model to the quality of service they deliver. If you can deliver exemplary service at work, you will be able to take this home with you.

There is a lot of excellent advice in Len Berry's book that well applies to the health care industry and the following are some pearls I've taken from his book and summarized here.

- Good service is about attitude. It 'sells' a promise but it isn't so much about making a promise as it is about keeping it. It is also about trust, which can only increase confidence in the 'customer' when the service is good. A major benefit in establishing trust, and this is never more true than in health care delivery, is that trust creates a reservoir of good will. The 'customer' is willing to forgive an error when it occurs, at least is more tolerant.
- If you are not happy with yourself, how can you expect the 'customer' to be happy. Or, if you are an unhappy physician, how do you expect your employees to be happy. Many employees don't leave their jobs but quit emotionally—they have abandoned the company but stay on the payroll. This rubs off on employees working with the disgruntled employee (which could easily be the physician), as well as the 'customer', who 'votes with his feet'.

- ♦ **You can't imitate good service!**

- Keep in mind that it is often the health care worker who must often bear the patient's disappointments and this includes receiving bad news about their health.
- Teamwork is one of the most beautiful experiences in life; it lifts the human spirit, creates energy and enthusiasm and brings a sense of pride. Pride in an organization brings joy and fun and the customer quickly picks up on this.

137

- The employee must be given the lee-way to innovate, that is, the authority to change what exists into something better, on the spot.
- Respect for everyone around you, including yourself, is the core value of every successful company. Work around the premise that *the customer is always right!*

Growth is always the by-word of any business, as it usually means profit. Berry has studied many companies and points out several features of 'success' that can ultimately be the ruin of any company:

1) Inspiration is jeopardized
2) Rules (bureaucracy) replaces informality
3) Turfism replaces teamwork
4) Memos and e-mails replace face-to-face communication
5) Supervisory layers replace impromptu visits and camaraderie
6) Sense of mission fades
7) Pride is diffused
8) Personal entrepreneurship and discretionary effort fades

♦ Success can create corporate arrogance!

Berry and Nita Bendapudi spent 4 months at Mayo Rochester and 1 month at Mayo Arizona, interviewing over 1000 patients and health care personnel including physicians in the process of evaluating our service delivery. They summarized what the ideal doctor that leads to the ideal doctor-patient encounter should be (I have mentioned almost all of these one way or another up to this point but worth repeating because this is why I wrote this book).

- A teacher, a partner. Kind, compassionate, humane and caring. Wants the best for the patient.
- Personal, interested in the patient as a person more than just a disease or a symptom. Remembers the patient.
- Empathetic, tries to understand what the patient is feeling and experiencing physically and emotionally.
- Respectful, trusts the patient to know his own body and feelings. Takes the patient's input seriously. Respects the patient's time and autonomy while including them as a partner in their own care.
- Thorough, conscientious and persistent.
- Forthright. Speaks to the patient honestly in a language he or she can understand.
- Confident. An assured manner inspires trust and gives the patient confidence in the care they are receiving.
- Communicates, listens to the patient and allows them to ask questions.
- Sensation of not being rushed.
- Timely continuity of care through a forthright manner.

This all results in greater patient, physician and staff satisfaction. This ultimately improves health measures outcome and reduces health care costs. The physician can't do any of the above without mutual respect for the patient.

It doesn't take much imagination to appreciate that what I've discussed regarding mutual respect also applies at home as well.

I would like to see all medical groups—private and academic—develop and publish for all to see a *Bill of Rights of Mutual Respect.*

STRESS*BURNOUT*DEPRESSION

Some stress is necessary as a form of motivation. It is inevitable. This is referred to as productive or creative stress. *Satisfied needs do not motivate.* A job without any stress would offer no challenge and likely be boring. *Dis-stress is a result of our thinking!* Stress becomes dysfunctional when it interferes with your life, when the demands of life exceed your coping abilities.

♦ **Stress is an ignorant state. It believes that everything is an emergency!** (Natalie Goldberg)

Just because you are a physician dealing with serious problems, putting in long hours, frustrations with paper work, impatience and resentment with normal patient demands, as well as an imbalance of life habits, doesn't mean you must succumb to all the problems around you. The personality traits that help young physicians acquire skills and accumulate facts—conscientiousness, compulsiveness, emotional control, an exaggerated commitment to your work, deferred gratification, a strong work ethic—are fostered and rewarded. But these are the same characteristics that predispose us to burnout, psychiatric illness, suicide, alcoholism, and drug abuse. Or, you feel victimized if people don't make something of your perceived sacrifices. *Stress leads to compassion fatigue!*

Just keeping up with the news is enough to depress one.

No man, woman or child is safe when
Congress is in session!
Will Rogers

Interestingly, more and more people are avoiding media news because it is so discouraging, and they say they feel better as a result.

There are 3 ways to approach stress: 1) prevent it, 2) ignore it and maybe it'll go away, and 3) deal with it. Number 2 is out. Since stress starts to build up in physicians in medical school and continues to do so throughout residency, this is the time to deal with it, or better yet, prevent it with coping mechanisms. We all rationalize that we don't have time to deal with it during these periods, or that it is 'normal' and will improve when we complete our training. But this isn't true. It can get worse and frequently does.

♦ **You must become the manager of your life, rather than a victim!**

As stated earlier, over 90% of medical students say they have been verbally abused during their 4 years of school, most commonly by residents and/or nurses. This is probably the first time in their lives that they have been at the bottom of the pecking order, and they have little or no recourse! Granted, many of these students might be extra sensitive, and 'stressed-out', but it is the perception that is important. Many feel they have lost some of their humanism as a result of this and certainly contributed to some of their stress, cynicism and callousness. To you medical students, you will soon be residents; remember to treat the medical students and junior residents how you wanted to be treated—with respect. It is up to you to break this cultural mean. And look at them as people, not just students.

Many medical schools and businesses offer help in dealing with stress but probably most people don't take advantage of it to the fullest, or at all—they don't have time for it! But, for the sake of yourself (remember, you are the most important person to you), your family and your patients, you must deal with the stress factors NOW.

Alvin Toffer says we are in an age of 'overchoices'. How many channels can you get on your TV? How many choices of red are there in the car you are considering buying— people lose sleep over these things. I'm old enough to remember when all cars were black. Henry Ford made it easy for car buyers: he said, "The public can have any color of car they want, as long as it is black!" Rather than enjoy the moment, we impulsively and then habitually pursue the next opportunity to make a choice. We underestimate the impact of the need to make choices has on complicating our lives. We have to live with the consequences of our choices. In one way or another we are subjected to more than 1000 ads per week; many of these are subliminal. Alas, the tremendous credit card debt in our country.

The advent of television advertising (over $100 billion per year) and later mail order catalogs, I think, were the start of our more stressful existence compared to the 'good old days'. Nearly 100% of advertising tells us what we are missing in life and that we'd be much happier if we bought what they are selling, and we can get it (happiness) NOW. Stress! As a result tens of millions of people are in huge debt. More stress!

If more is better, we will never have enough. *Enough* should become a by-word in your life. It helps simplify your life. We have too much already! So what if your peers have seemingly 'gotten ahead'. Are they truly happy? As I've said before, learn to say to yourself, *So what!*

♦ **There must be more to life than having everything!** (Maurice Sendak)

The advertisers offer expectations that can't be met—you can't buy happiness. Want becomes need, luxury becomes a necessity. Our decisions to get more become non-discerning, passive, impulsive. We've lost control. More stress!

Saying *thank you* appropriately and genuinely inculcates a sense of gratitude, and in turn, happiness, in the person repeatedly saying it. This is stress reducing.

Speed contributes to stress—we're all in a big hurry, driving faster, to get somewhere a few minutes sooner. All the while releasing stress-associated endorphins. Then our racing motor can't slow down for hours. In the meantime, we eat more and faster. More stress! Hurrying becomes a habit, an opioid, countering serenity and inner tranquility. You can't have it both ways!

♦ **Anxiety is the space between 'now' and 'then', what I have referred to as 'pretraumatic stress syndrome'!**

Balance and simplification of your life as well as your philosophy towards life and work, including spirituality, your relationships and self-care, all combined, can make a huge difference in your response to stress. And remember—*don't take yourself too seriously!* At the same time you need to remember that life isn't always fair and this is true for everyone. Life is 3 steps forward and 1 back. Philosophers from the Eastern societies say that we in Western societies have become sheltered from suffering and that when it occurs, we have trouble handling it. We don't know how to face it. For some, suffering can overwhelm the mind. But, suffering is a part of life. Dealing with it strengthens us and makes us more understanding and compassionate, as well as more tolerant of adversities and challenges when they occur, and they will occur! It's been said that the more problems we have and deal with, the stronger we will be. Frankl points out that once a person has a reason to be happy, he is more capable of coping with suffering. However, we can't change ourselves overnight; *it takes at least 3 to 4 weeks, and probably longer, to change almost any personal thing—a habit, a mind-think, a pattern of living*. Accept the fact that it will take awhile. And don't try to change too many things at once—take one at a time!

We are creatures of habit and sometimes our habits are so ingrained and strong that it won't allow us to accept change. *You can't change what you won't acknowledge*. Fighting change can be tremendously stressful. The best way to handle this, when possible, is to be a part of the change. It must be your choice. If we are to improve on our qualities, especially our attitude, then we will need to change, albeit, slowly.

♦ **Life is just one damn thing after another!** (Elbert Hubbard)

I would change this to "…….multiple damn things after another."

Stress is an accumulative thing. It ultimately leads to burnout and burnout to chemical depression. You can argue that true depression leads to burnout and I don't disagree with that, as I pointed out early on that 15 to 25% of the population (maybe higher in physicians) will ultimately develop chemical depression (I refer to chemical depression as a condition that responds to anti-depressants versus a depression that also needs some psychotherapy).

♦ **The only trouble with success is that the formula for achieving it is the same as the formula for a nervous breakdown!** (Chuck Swindoll)

The World Health Organization estimates that in the developed countries by 2020 depression will be the 2nd leading cause of disability after heart disease. Depression doesn't appreciably shorten the life span, in fact, you'll just feel like life drags on forever! However, add depression to a chronic illness and it will shorten the life span.

♦ **Every morning I get up and read the obituaries and if my name isn't there, I feel better for a while!** (Oscar Levant)

Various studies show that over half of all physicians suffer from some form of burnout (in a survey of internal medicine residents, three-quarters met the criteria for stress and in half of these it was bad enough to affect their work performance). There is no joy, spontaneity or affection. They feel that they are undervalued, and probably are. *Emotional exhaustion* is the hallmark of burnout, all reserve is gone. This results in a *depersonalization* as a defense measure against further emotional drain and ultimately a *decreased sense of personal accomplishment*—"Why am I here? No one seems to care!" Cynicism affects every thought and action. Doing anything for fun produces more guilt and is looked on as a waste of time. They lose interest in everything, and ultimately suffer an emotional shutdown. They become 'emotionally unavailable' to themselves and everyone else. Absolutely nothing good can come out of this for the patient's sake or for the family. These physicians are a source of many medical errors, some disastrous and most preventable. Early recognition of the state of distress of this physician is imperative so that action can be taken.

♦ **It's hard to fight an enemy who has outposts in your head!**

Emotional exhaustion doesn't happen overnight and is the culmination of many things, beginning in medical school where the student, later the resident, are unprepared for the emotional demands put upon them, leaving them feeling drained. I'm certain that sleep deprivation plays a major role in many cases. There is a tendency to compete with peers in getting to work earlier or staying up later, or both, to work on a paper, prepare a report, etc. Yet we all require different amounts of sleep every night and it is the rare individual who gets by with only 4 hours of sleep. Emulating this produces a start on a slippery slope.

Perceived (or actual) loss of control is one of the major causes of burnout. The professional expects with all this training that he or she should be in complete control. It is the unrealization of this expectation that leads to their downfall. However, remember *you do have control of your attitude*!

♦ **It is not a sign of weakness to ask for help!**

In fact, people will think more of you if you ask for help than if you don't. For we men, that is hard to understand. Caring for yourself isn't selfish. *We are not in this alone!*

Depersonalization as a defense measure is an attitude of detached concern leading to arrogance and callousness and cynicism. And this isn't only with patients but with his or her health care worker associates and eventually the family. Some physicians try to compensate by working harder, namely longer hours rather than smarter, and this becomes a treadmill existence. It is estimated that up to 10% of health professionals develop substance abuse as a result.

At this point a sense of diminished personal accomplishment takes over, which I think is a state of depression. You no longer enjoy anything, including your family, or of gratification of truly helping someone, of saving lives! You're not having fun. You've lost any sense of humor you might have had. Your ability to apply wisdom is impaired. And certainly you aren't happy. Everything begins to fall apart. Now you really need some help. Some like to refer to this as a mid-life crisis. However, many people, not just physicians, anticipate the coming burnout or are in the early phases of it, and decide to make a career change or location change. And for many it works, but for others it doesn't. This has to be well thought out, and maybe with some professional help.

Preventing and dealing with stress and burnout are similar and require a concerted effort on your part; it should become a part of your life, not just a temporary measure. These measures should begin early in life, but it is never too late. Remember, *There has never been a documented case report of a person saying on their death bed, "Gee, I wish I had spent more time at the office!"*

There are thousands of books, lay articles and articles in medical journals, and a multitude of lectures and courses on dealing with stress, but common sense will tell you what most of these are—you just need to find the ones that you are comfortable with and enjoy.

The following are some obvious and maybe not so obvious ways of *preventing/dealing with stress and burnout*. These are coping skills and not in any particular order of importance.

- A *balanced life* is one of the most important things you can do in practicing the Art of Living. I can't repeat this often enough. This includes a balance of your inner motives with your external actions.

  - **The greater the balance, the greater the joy, energy and creativity!** (Ann McGee-Cooper)

  - **Your work is not your life, it is a part of your life!** (Anne Quinlan)

- Practice the Art of Living—**FAMILY, FRIENDS, FUN, FELLOWSHIP, FAITH, FORGIVE AND FORGET!**
- Read Carlson's book on *Don't Sweat The Small Things, And They Are All Small Things.* Write down key suggestions and read them every so often. Remember, a year from now, most of the things you do or don't do won't be remembered. What will you accomplish by going 120%--will you respect yourself? *Instead, work smart!* Practice *time management.*
- *Learn to say **NO** and do it gracefully.* This is the ultimate in self-care. Have a prepared legitimate excuse like, "I promised my family I wouldn't take on any more until I get some other things done first," or, "I really appreciate you thinking of me but maybe next year."

  - **My answer is 'maybe' and that's final!**

- **NO** is one of the few words that can't be misunderstood. It is easier to say *No* now and *Yes* later than the reverse.
- Practice mindfulness—don't delve in the past or the future. Critical!

  - **Worry does not empty tomorrow of its problems. It only empties today of its strength!**

- Put mistakes made out of your mind after you've dealt with them and learned from them. Then move on. Psychologists have shown that people can forcibly be able to forget the past uncomfortable events. Writing this out may help (see section on Write-Therapy below). However, I'm impressed some people don't want to forget these—they thrive on them. *They're victims of themselves!* How can they practice blame if they don't have a negative event around which to focus on!

  - **If you don't learn from your mistakes, why make them!**

  > **A life spent making mistakes is not only more**
  > **Honorable but more useful than a life**
  > **Spent doing nothing!**
  > **George Bernard Shaw**

- Have a mentor(s), not someone to ventilate your personal problems to, but someone that 'has been there' and can guide you around the pitfalls. Ideally, it should be someone who will recognize when you are stretched.
- Cultivate within yourself a 'self awareness' which I also call social as well as emotional intelligence. This is your ability to appropriately interact with everyone and everything around you, and to appreciate what your 'being' is to these people. You might call this 'enhanced personal awareness', mindfulness. Be a part of life, don't fight it, but don't allow people to take

advantage of you. Take control of your life. Expectations by others has a powerful effect on how we run our lives. Beware of this.

- Have good friends and not necessarily other physicians, or in the same profession or business as you are, and 2 or 3 friends you can confide in. Nurture these friendships. Ideally, one of these would be your spouse. *To have friends, you have to be one*. Women develop this skill better than men. The essence of family and friends is a harbor of safety and sanctity. Shutting off connectedness leads to or aggravates depression.
- *Celebrate*. Celebrate everything you can. Socialize on a regular basis; *always have something fun to look forward to*. I think this is an unappreciated source of happiness *today!*
- Know your limitations—everyone has them. Work around them. We only have to be good at most things, not the best in everything.
- Exercise regularly. It's a good anti-depressant and it takes your mind off things.
- Promote collegiality among your peers. This acts as a support group, but don't let it become pure gripe sessions.
- A formal support system that meets regularly where you share concerns and develop positive solutions can be very effective.
- Precious solitude for 20 minutes a day is invaluable. At a minimum **pause** for 2 to 3 minutes, several times during the day, preferably without distractions and think of nothing, or, of very good thoughts. Work on your happiness intentions. Look at a picture of your family. Take some deep breaths. More people are aware of the weather forecast than they are the tension in their bodies. After this is a good time to drink some fluids.

- ♦ **All miseries derive from not being able to sit quietly in a room alone!** (Blaise Pascal)

- ♦ **The best time to relax is when you don't have time for it!**

- **Sleep!** I'm repeating this again! There is absolutely no substitute for this in the long run. Staying up more hours per day doesn't mean you are getting more out of life. On the contrary, it may be very counterproductive. Assessing your need for this should be high priority. You may have to forego your favorite late night show or night news. And when going to sleep, limit your thoughts to one thing, one positive thing. A flight of many thoughts over-stimulates the brain.

- ♦ **Studies repeatedly show the powerful negative effects of fatigue and illness on effective decision making!** (Stephen Covey)

- Procrastination is an energy drainer. I've discussed this earlier. One predictor of future depression is indecisiveness. *Learn to make prompt decisions and then live with them*. Don't second guess yourself. Handle the most difficult, but necessary, problems first.
- *Learn to want what you have*. Seek peace of mind and contentment.
- **Laugh every day.** Laughing is like yawning—it can be infectious. It is a tremendous stress reliever.
- Take a day off every week where you don't think medicine or about your job and don't feel guilty about it! You'll be more productive as a result.
- Develop hobbies including reading. There aren't many situations like getting lost in a good book you can't put down to take your mind off things. But be

cautious on letting hobbies and exercise become too goal oriented. RELAX! HAVE FUN!

- Practice **Write-Therapy** (see below).
- *Avoid all negative thoughts!* Negative thoughts create negative behavior. We become what we think, what we do!

  ♦ **He mastered the fine art of whining!** (Woody Allen)

- *Think positive!* A Mayo study by Maruta et al published in the Mayo Clinic Proceedings showed that pessimism is associated with a nearly 20% increased risk of mortality compared to optimism. If pessimism affects your mortality, what does it do for your psyche!

  ♦ **An optimist thinks that this is the best possible world while a pessimist fears that this is true!**

- Don't let your weekly periodicals pile up, if this frustrates you. Don't renew those you don't look at. For the physician, rip your medical journals and keep the articles or just the abstracts you want. Looking at a pile of unread journals and magazines everyday is stressful.
- Avoid associating with negative people.
- Don't try to be someone else. You are unique. Build on this. It takes courage to be yourself.
- Stress lowers the threshold to anger. Find ways of dealing with your anger, hopefully before the situation arises. Holding onto anger is extremely stressful, affects sleep and takes you away from mindfulness, and is an energy drainer. And you lose some control and your values. For some people anger produces an excitement, a high. It may be the only excitement in their lives and they live by it.
- Practice time efficiency. Minimize interruptions. Handle a paper or document only once—deal with it. Be organized—get help with this if necessary—but not over organized; need balance here. Be decisive. But remember, life is made up of interruptions; you must accept this.
- Deadlines are one of the most common causes of stress.

  ♦ **Our greatest weariness comes from work not done!** (Eric Hoffer)

- Don't confuse *urgent* with *important*. Is someone or something creating the urgency? Has the feeling of urgency made it feel important? Many activities become urgent as a result of lack of preparation. Urgency becomes addicting. We go from one 'urgent' crisis to the next.
- Practice calmness, equanimity, tranquillity, serenity. Learn to relax—concentrate on this. Slow down! Meditation, yoga and other means can be very effective for some people.
- Stopping something that is stressful can be an option—why not?
- Is noise pollution a part of your life? Are you able to go at least 5 straight minutes during the day with complete silence? Does the music you listen to hype you up when what you need is something to calm you down? Do you automatically turn on the TV when you come home? Even though you're not especially watching it? Practice quietness—may take some time to get used to it, probably at least 3 to 4 weeks.
- *Don't take yourself too seriously.*
- Take care of your physical and mental health. Get regular exams.

- Drink plenty of fluids. Some feel that stress and exhaustion are aggravated by chronic dehydration.
- Go out of your way to compliment someone. Do volunteer work.

♦ **Do something for someone who can never repay you!**

- Accept compliments gracefully. Then write the good ones down and look at them occasionally.
- Be grateful for high moods and graceful in low moods; everyone has these swings—they're normal! I repeat, they are normal! Accept this. Without the low moods, we wouldn't appreciate the high ones. The simple act of acknowledging a low-state of mind, knowing we are temporarily seeing life in a distorted way allows us to stop overanalyzing things until our mood rises, and it will! *The lowest ebb is the turn of the tide.* We are allowed to be grumpy now and then, but you can break out of this mood faster by smiling, by a little act of kindness, giving a compliment. Understand other people when they are in a low mood—learn to sense this and support them. But don't let their low mood ruin your day. And don't let your low mood ruin someone else's day!
- Caution on making major decisions during low mood times, and certainly banish negative thoughts. Don't allow passing negative thoughts to become thought attacks.
- Talk to yourself. Give yourself a pep talk. Be positive. Review a list of your strengths. Remember, *this too, shall pass.*
- *Be the best you can be*, then relax.
- **Smile.** Act cheerful; pretty soon it will become a habit.
- Nurture yourself.
- Back off, slow down your pace of life and work when you feel stressed. Exercise. Find quiet time.

♦ **You must withdraw completely every now and then to restore or replete your inner energy and resources!**

- Do not allow yourself to become isolated.
- Relinquish some control.
- Deal with one thing at a time—this is mindfulness.
- If you are in debt, get expert help now to manage this.
- Spirituality may give you some outs on how to reduce stress.
- Always maintain an aura of hope, which is a belief in the goodness of people and that good things will happen while bad things won't last long.
- Take all your vacation time and use it to have fun. *The real problem with your leisure time and activity is how to keep other people from using it.*

♦ **Just because someone throws you a ball doesn't mean you have to catch it!** (Richard Carlson)

- Learn to temper your estimations of things. Under and over estimations lead to expectations that can't be met—stressful.
- If you are in academia, an HMO or group practice, or associated with a large business or even a service club, ask to have a stress management and a time-efficiency course. A session on happiness!
- Seek maturity and wisdom.

- Be yourself. Don't try to be someone else. This takes courage. Life is what you are!
- Know when to seek help and do it!
- Delegate.
- **FAMILY, FRIENDS, FUN, FELLOWSHIP, FAITH, FORGIVE & FORGET!** I'm repeating this to emphasize their importance.
- Don't hold a grudge—forgive! Many of the things I read in preparing for this book point out that the ability to forgive is one of the most important determinants to happiness. Bitterness is an illusion that you are fighting your misfortunes. Forgiving is a gift you give yourself—it cleanses the mind and doesn't allow prior events to create anger. It doesn't mean you have to abolish the event from your mind after you've dealt with it, but you've subjugated it to a place of lesser importance.

    ◆ **When everyone is out to get you, paranoia is only smart thinking!**

- **Forgive yourself!** It's an act of kindness.
- You can't please everyone—accept this. It's 100%!
- It's OK to feel good when things go bad.
- Learn resilience. In times of adversity the critical determinant of success in life and business is resilience, but don't become thick skinned, non-caring. I call this *sensitive resilience,* another form of balance in your life. Remember, it is what you think of yourself that is important, not what others think.
- Smyth et al found that by asking a group of patients with asthma or rheumatoid arthritis to write for 20 minutes a day for 3 days about emotionally traumatic events in their lives, they significantly improved their health status compared to the control group (see Write-Therapy below). It's worth thinking about, especially for men who are otherwise reluctant to express their feelings openly.

    ◆ **There is nothing harder on a person's health than being stressed over past matters that are no longer worthy of concern!**

- As you get older, interact socially with people younger than you; this brings you 'up' to their level of energy and thinking, and can truly make you think and feel younger.

    ◆ **The idea is to die young as late as possible!** (Ashley Montagu)

- Ask yourself, *What is really important?* then write it down. **Have some Fun!**
- Seek help from a Life Coach. These are people trained to get people's lives straightened out, but this is not psychotherapy. Many are licensed. Most do this via phone conversations, for a price.

Simplify your life! A brief discussion on simplifying your life can lead to a major reduction in your stress. Many authors including Elaine St James and Paul Borthwick and Donna Smallin have made a living telling us what we already know on uncomplicating our lives. I know of no books written on how to complicate our lives— we have television for that. Our lives border on chaos, with so many uncertainties that our stress is pushed to the maximum. It has been stated that in a lifetime a person will need to learn how to use 20,000 different items, anywhere from a pencil sharpener to more computer attachments, to maybe even things I can't imagine.

- **A man is rich in proportion to the things he can do without!** (Henry David Thoreau)

Thoreau also said as far back as 1850, "....our life is frittered away in detail!" and that the more we simplify our life "the laws of the universe will appear less complex."

- **No matter what happens, somebody will find a way to take it too seriously!** (Dave Berry)

In addition to TV advertising, we have catalogs, the Internet, malls and shopping TV networks *to show us things we didn't know we didn't need and buying it anyway to impress people we don't care about!* Buying feeds arrogance and greed and low self-esteem.

Begin to simplify your life by cutting way back on passively watching TV and do things you enjoy doing with this extra time. Watching TV begets more mindlessness. The average adult watches 4 hours of TV daily. Delay buying non essentials until the urge passes; the more you buy the more you have to take care of. Minimize your obligations. Remember, the ability to say NO is crucial.

- **How you spend your days is how you spend your life!**

Practice mindfulness in your relaxing hours as well as at work. This will allow you to more fully enjoy the little things in life, bypassing the need for the 'big things' that are ultimately less rewarding, more expensive and more time consuming and less memorable. Try to visualize what it would take to simplify your life, write it down, then begin doing it. Or, seek help from books like those of St James, Borthwick and Smallin. The whole household has to cooperate in this venture.

One secret in simplifying your life, and I've alluded to it already a few times, and that is the value of *silence*. We're afraid of it! A few moments of extreme quiet makes us nervous and we start thinking. If our thinking is in the negative mode, our mind will bring up things we don't want to think about, resulting in us quickly turning on the radio or TV.

In the quiet solitude you will hear
The voice of wisdom!

To acquire the ability to 'tolerate' silence, you have to sneak up on it. It takes discipline. Begin by sitting quietly and relaxed for 1 minute. Then gradually over a period of days and week increase this up to 20 or 30 minutes. You don't have to meditate but you must have positive thoughts; look at some pictures of loved ones or places. Pretty soon you will look forward to these moments of quiet peace. If you work in a noisy, bustling place, see if the manager won't consider a quiet room to retreat to at your break.

- **Silence is sometimes the best answer!**

In putting the material together for this book, I eventually realized that a feature of emotional intelligence, happiness, self-esteem, equanimity, wisdom and maturity is *not to expect too much of other people; then you won't be disappointed or stressed.*

- **I realize now how precious each day is!** (cancer survivor)

Write-Therapy. In reviewing a number of different topics on *The Art of Living...The Art of Medicine* I am impressed how often I've come across the recommendation of putting your thoughts on paper—*successful people think on paper!* Some call this 'journaling'. Henriette Klauser's *Write It Down, Make It Happen,* Phillip McGraw's *Self Matters,* James Pennebaker's *Opening Up. The Healing Power of Expressing Emotions,* Susan Zimmerman's *Writing to Heal the Soul. Transforming Grief and Loss Through Writing,* and two books I have already mentioned, Foster and Hicks' *How We Choose to Be Happy*, and Crenshaw's *The Art of Living* highlight the importance of journaling. Their messages revolve around 'writing it down'.

It's likely that writing rather than just thinking about the problem or situation "re-hard wires" your brain with actual neurochemical changes, producing lasting imprints in the brain, including the subconscious. (Remember, your subconscious is working 24 hours a day). It requires mindfulness to do this, causing you to think even more about the event. Writing it out, externalizing your inner thoughts, makes it more real; it acts as a cathartic, and is a form of meditation for some people. Your thoughts go into slow motion, at least slower than they are when only in the thinking mode. And you're not likely to lie to yourself when journaling.

You must put "I" in your entries, otherwise you are avoiding responsibility for your thoughts. I've mentioned most of my ideas as well as the authors I've listed above, throughout the book but I think worth repeating here since it may be an effective means of managing your life and dealing with stress. This is best done in quiet solitude, with semidarkness contributing to an aura of anonymity, if necessary.

Just thinking or talking about these isn't nearly as effective as writing it. I don't know if hand writing is better than using the computer. I don't look at this as a diary detailing daily events, but as a written personalized journal of you. Keep in mind that it is likely to be read by family members some day, even if you hide it, unless you destroy what you don't want seen before you die. However, my idea is that most or all of this, except #14, you will want to share with others.

1) Begin by writing on your *philosophy of life.* This exercise will really make you think and can be a maturing process. It helps set your priorities. Everyone has a philosophy of life, don't they? No. And though you may have thought briefly about it, it doesn't take a life of its own, at least not as effectively, until you put it in writing. Maybe you did this years ago as an assignment in school, but it is worth revisiting again. As I discussed in the section on happiness, Prager thinks our philosophy of life must include how we <u>will</u> handle the normal, but sometimes serious, setbacks of life. Writing this down will bring some clarity and focus to these events, which you can count on occurring. Remember, suffering is a part of life.

♦ **A change imposed is a change opposed!** (Spencer Johnson)

Happiness must be more than a goal in life, it must be a philosophy of daily living. You need to work on this in nearly everything you do. Begin by writing out:

A) What truly makes me happy? Do this rapidly in 3 minutes.
B) What do I need to do to achieve happiness?

C) What is my attitude? How can I improve on it?

Writing this out is the start on the road to being happy, which may take months and years but don't get discouraged; it will come. *Remember, the reason to be alive is to enjoy it.*

Your philosophy of life becomes your personal mission statement. As you write these out, ask yourself these questions:

A) Am I open to new ideas or do I keep a closed mind?
B) Can I aggressively make my own decisions, promptly, or do I passively wait for others to do this for me?
C) Do I accept myself as I am while always striving to improve myself, or am I frustrated by my and others' imperfections? And expectations?
D) Do I operate on assumptions?
E) Am I passionate and excited about life and its challenges, or do I see it as a struggle? Again, what is my attitude?

2) Next, list *what is really important to you,* in order of importance. Carry this list with you and look at it every so often as it will help you keep your life in perspective and in balance. At the bottom of the list, write *Learn to say NO, Don't sweat the small things,* and *Ignore the unimportant.*

3) *What are your goals?*, besides being happy every day, your short and long term goals? Your 5 year plan? This is your vision statement. These goals will change and thus need periodic updating but it will give you some guidance in an organized format. List your priorities within the goals. At the top of the list write BALANCE, followed by FAMILY, FRIENDS, FUN, FAITH, FORGIVE, FORGET......Work. Then begin your list. You will need to remind yourself every so often of the order of priority these deserve. You can add to your list what you think it will take to attain these. It is not necessary you obtain all your goals (beyond balance, and the 6 Fs), or within the time frame you set.

After listing each of your goals which can include things besides your job such as hobbies, physical conditioning, improving how you feel about yourself, etc., write out as many things you see as necessary to attain these goals.

4) *List your blessings.* The length of this list may surprise you. Keep adding to this list as you think of more things and carry this list with you as well as in your journal. Then, write out the following: "I am glad that I'm not......" and do this for several things like, "I am glad that my tests showed no cancer," or, "I'm glad that my child doesn't have xxxx disease like so and so's child," or, "I'm glad I didn't accept the chair of that committee." The list can be lengthy. *What you escaped can be as rewarding as what you got.*

5) *Who am I?* Begin by listing all your good qualities. Rate them 1 to 4, with '4' being the highest. How would you want the clergy or your friends to remember you at your funeral? They aren't interested in the estate you left, the cost of your car or the monthly fees at the country club. Don't be humble here. This list is different than the one on your goals—it is more personal. Below are a list of qualities and conditions to begin with and then

add your own that I have overlooked. Which ones need work; list how to do this. This becomes your guidelines for *continuous personal improvement*. Tackle only a few at a time; I can't emphasize this enough. Trying to do ten will discourage you and you won't do any! Improvement comes in small, almost imperceptible, increments, not big ones.

Balance	Family, Friends, Fun	Forgive, Forget
Happiness/joy	Decisiveness	Integrity
Loving	Gratitude	Equanimity
Kindness	Self-esteem	Positive attitude
Think	Simplified life style	Seek wisdom/maturity
Caring	Volunteer	Communicate/listen
Humility	Role model	Seek happiness
Civility	Hope	Sense of humor
Deep listener	Grateful	Passion for life
Respectful	Good wellness concept	Tolerant
Optimistic	Honest/trustworthy	Sensitive resilience
Productive	Emotional intelligence	Intuitive
Mindful	Compassionate	Fellowship
Creative	Spiritual	A smiler
Understanding	Celebrate	A peace of mind
Empathetic	Pride in work/appearance	Dignified
Love of nature	Enthusiastic	Sincere
Independent	Desire to learn, to grow	Warm
Responsible	Courageous	Loyal
Persistent	Self-disciplined	Hard worker

6) *Happy moments,* memorable events, compliments received, accomplishments. As I stated earlier some of these remain in your active memory bank for only a few weeks so you should write them down on a card you carry with you and transcribe them into your journal (computer, if you wish). In later years looking back on these in your journal will bring back fantastic memories. Make a scrapbook of your accomplishments. I photograph my diplomas, certificates, etc., to an 8 ½ x 11 format and put them in a scrapbook along with nice letters, photographs and other memorabilia. (What is your family going to do with a box of framed certificates?). List your favorite accomplishments and describe them.

7) *List things you really enjoy doing.* What gives you energy? If you aren't already doing most of these, then start now. What would you like to do if it were impossible to fail?

8) *List 50 to 100 things you would like to do before you die.* What's keeping you from doing these? Put an asterisk beside those that are doable if money and time weren't a problem. Underline those that you would really regret not doing. What would you do if you were a billionaire?

9) *Time management!* What can you do to improve your time efficiency? Do something! Outline this on paper—you'll be surprised where you can begin making changes, but usually only after seeing this written down.

10) *Simplify your life!* This will help your time efficiency, your happiness, reduce your stress, and more. List the ways you can begin doing this and then do it. Update this regularly.

11) *What's worrying you? What are your fears?* What are the major causes of stress in your life? After each one, list 2 or 3 things you can try to do about it. **BE HAPPY!**

12) *What can you do to reduce stress and be happier, today?* After listing these begin working on them within your goals listed under #3. What do you need to do to change?

13) *Major decisions in your life.* We all have these to make. Listing the pros and cons and assigning a value to each of these can put them in perspective only after seeing them before you and looking at them several times before making the decision.

14) *Life disturbing events:* Mistakes made, disappointments, involvement in a car accident or lawsuit, marital discord, something you feel *guilty* about. Situations you are grieving over. What really made me appreciate the value of writing out things is what I mentioned earlier where people with asthma or rheumatoid arthritis got measurably and subjectively better by writing about emotionally disturbing events for 20 minutes a day for 3 days, as compared to the control group with the same disease but who wrote about very benign thoughts. (I don't know whether or not you can do this in one 45 to 60 minute session rather than three). Then destroy the paper. Write as fast as you can, letting the thoughts flow. Elaine St. James in her book *Inner Simplicity* suggests writing with the non dominant hand if you can do this, as this lets the 'right brain', the intuitive side, take over. This begins the process of *forgiving and forgetting,* a closure process. Some things you will never forget or never be able to fix, but writing it seems to help deal with it better and maybe take the edge off. You can repeat this as often as you feel it helps you.

Pennebaker approached this a little differently, by doing a number of studies that monitored physiologic responses. He then followed the health care needs of many college students as a way of monitoring their health. The following summarizes what he learned about the healing power of expressing emotions, including the writing (confessing your emotions by linking your thoughts and your feelings) of things disturbing to you:

- Reduces your physiologic hyperresponsiveness (remember, I mentioned some of these in the section on The Science of Caring).
- Overcomes denial and inhibition while promoting self understanding and insight.
- Improves physical health, gives a peace of mind and improves immune function, with all these parameters lasting 6 weeks to four months.
- Acts as an antidepressant, pointing out that all this is more difficult if you are already depressed. However, this doesn't mean you should not try it. He does point out that for a few hours after confessional-writing, you might feel momentarily depressed.

- By doing this, the memory has been preserved (even if you throw the paper away) and there is now less reason to rehearsing the event actively.

15) *Grieving,* obviously, is one of the most personal things we can go through. Talking about it as we go through the 5 processes (see section on End of Life issues) is therapeutic. However, after a while, there is no one to talk to about it, again, but the grieving goes on, for some longer than others. Writing a letter to your deceased love one also has great healing powers. You can deal with some of the negative issues in this letter as well. All this can be done as often and as long as necessary. It is a way of sharing your grief, maybe with your subconscious.

   ♦ **You must remember, suffering is the one promise life always keeps!** (U. Aung Ko)

16) *Open letter to your employees/customers/patients.* This is a form of a newsletter. In medicine we are all frustrated with the external demands put upon us. As I have stated before I think our patients could be our best allies but not unless they are informed. We need to give our side and this could be done in a quarterly letter to our patients put in the waiting room. It must be objective, non self-serving, not bitter, just the facts. We don't have time to talk to each individual patient about why we are allotted only 15 minutes a visit, why we are constrained from doing certain tests, about government regulations, etc.

17) *Future letter to your children or grandchildren.* Within a year after each of my 2 grandchildren were born, I wrote them a long letter to be opened on their 13th birthday, on the chance I might not be around. I told them a lot of the things I have put into this book (it was from this idea that got me started on this book) as well as some other things about dating, school, values, etc. It is in a safe deposit box waiting for them. Keep a copy in your journal and add to it if you wish. Remember, *there is no such thing as a wise young man!*

18) *Your life history.* For years I have told my senior patients who at times told me they didn't think they were contributing much, that they ought to be writing their life history, going back to their very first memories. Fifty, one hundred, two hundred years from now it will be a living legacy of you, listing the hardships you endured without TV, a computer, SUVs, car turn signals, infomercials, remote controls. Include everything you know about your ancestors. Make it as long as you wish. Pay a grandchild to write it up on the word processor if you don't type.

19) *Current resume′ or curriculum vitae (CV).* This is your obituary! Update it regularly.

20) *Advanced Directive.* Keep a copy here in your journal as well as other secure places. If your family knows about your journal (maybe you already shared it with them), they will know where a copy of your Advanced Directive is, should you be suddenly ill.

21) *Lists.* There was a period of time when we made fun of each other for keeping lists of things we needed to do, to buy, to see, to the point that some of us were embarrassed to be seen relying on lists. But life has become so complicated that I have become a believer in lists. It helps in time management and simplifying your life. If a list saves you 30 minutes or more a week, in a year that is at least a day in your life. Write it down or put it in your PDA. Everyone has to come up with their own formula. *Think on paper!*

**Hard work doesn't burn us out,
Joylessness burns us out!**
**LL Berry &
N Bendapudi**

END OF LIFE ISSUES

**It is impossible that anything so natural, so necessary,
And so unusual as death should ever have
Been designed as an evil to mankind!
Jonathan Swift**

We all know that we'll eventually die. What most people don't appreciate is that many physicians see this as a failure on their part! We have been taught—and the public has come to expect this—that through advanced technology and superior pharmacology, that we the physicians can keep almost anyone alive. What this really means is that we can prolong dying, not living. And we are dying lonelier!

♦ **Thinking about death produces a love for life!** (Albert Schweitzer)

The spiritual dimensions of dying bonds persons together—the patient, the family, friends and health care personnel who cared for the patient. In a perverse sort of way it can make those people involved in the death a little bit better people through a shared suffering and appreciate all the more the value of life.

When there is no victory for the physician, when the challenge is gone (prolonging dying is frequently seen as the ultimate challenge), the physician loses interest; death is against everything they've been trained for. Sad. It is frequently easier and less time consuming for the physician to initiate life sustaining measures, wasting limited resources, than to discuss the situation with the patient and/or the family. Subconsciously, or even consciously, the physician knows that he will be paid for instituting these measures but probably not for sitting with the patient or family. Not uncommonly previously completed Advanced Directives are lost or forgotten about, and the details poorly recalled by the family.

♦ **Doctors have an imbalance between caring and curing!**

Too many physicians work on the assumption that if they can't cure the disease, their job is done! There is even an element of this among some nurses who tend to answer the call light of other patients before that of the terminally ill patient.

**The true test of the physician is
When he or she must comfort without the hope of a cure!**

If the patient does respond to the heroic measures, will he ever leave the hospital? What will his quality of life be? I'm concerned that in teaching hospitals if there is a 'trend', a 'cultural mean' by the attendings to be heroic rather than individualize each situation, this becomes the norm for the residents and perpetuated. It becomes a part of the institutional culture, with the patient preferences ignored. Unless, of course, death is imminent, then the physician(s) disappears. I'm not standardizing all physicians as acting this way; on the contrary, the majority are very caring. But it is the ones who are indifferent and non caring that has become the reputation for the rest of us.

However, it is not always the physician's fault as not rarely, keeping heroic measures going is at one or more members of the family's urging, possibly to assuage guilt, or out of anger.

♦ **The secret of life is to know when enough is enough!** (Vincent Ryan)

Because of all this we have a tremendous problem in this country (much less so than in the developing countries and even the developed nations where health care is rationed). In the USA 1% of the population dies every year (2.5 to 3.0 million people). Probably only about 5% of us die acutely, within minutes of an event. Further facts about the end of life include:

- 90% of people want to die at home; less than 25% do. Over 60% of deaths occur in acute care hospitals rather than at home or a hospice.
- Over 35% spend at least 10 days in intensive care.
- Up to ½ of total lifetime health care costs occur in the last 6 to 8 weeks of a person's life.
- 1/3 bankrupt their families as a result of prolonged dying.
- Less than one-half of clergy have training in dealing with end of life issues.
- Only 20% of physician's prediction of survival time are reasonably accurate.
- 50% to 80% of dying patients with pain receive inadequate pain control (including children!), and at least 1/3 of their emotional distress is not dealt with or inadequately managed (I suspect it is higher than this).
- Nearly 2/3 are cared for in their final days by a physician(s) they have known for less than one week.

♦ **Someone I barely know is about to tell me if I'm going to die!**

Much of this wouldn't happen if the patient had completed an Advanced Directive and 1) given a copy to his or her doctor, 2) given copies to each member of the immediate family, 3) taken a copy to the hospital or nursing home with them, and 4) traveled with one. It's not enough to just have a copy, it is imperative to discuss your wishes with your family and your doctor. The physician must take the lead in encouraging all his or her patients to complete one.

Advanced Directives can be either a *Living Will, Durable Power of Attorney, or Health Care Proxy,* which is also called a surrogate decision maker.

♦ **We spend more time learning how to run our VCR than we do on how we want the end of our life to be managed!**

Overall, about 20% of the adult population have completed an Advanced Directive but many of these people don't even know where a copy is! Over 2/3 of those over age 65 have an Advanced Directive but less than 20% have shared it with their doctor. And only about 1/3 of those selected to be surrogates knew they were selected!

As I stated earlier I think all medical students ought to complete an Advanced Directive in their freshman year and go over it with the physician who conducts their physical exam. It will make them more empathetic to their patients and they can say they've completed one—as well as an organ donor declaration.

Advanced Directives are about formalizing a way for you to share your end of life concerns with your physician and your family. It also gives you an opportunity to think about what you truly want when you become seriously ill, which could be tomorrow or 3 or 50 or more years hence. The terms of the Advanced Directive can be changed any time. And I suggest re-doing it or resigning and dating it every so often such as every 4 years, maybe on national election day, or February 29th.

If a mentally clear person hasn't thought things out ahead of time and is now acutely confronted with a possible life threatening crisis, it is much more difficult for him to refuse interventional life maintaining measures until he has time to reason through what is happening with himself, his family and his physician.

Advanced Directives are pretty simple when you realize that what it is asking for is 1) death with dignity without suffering, even if you request heroic measures, and 2) a 'shared-control' with the physician(s), a maintenance of your autonomy.

♦ **Preparation does not preclude hope!**

Essentially no one wants to be kept alive while in a vegetative state, yet this could happen without an Advanced Directive, and especially if the person hasn't discussed his wishes with all his children. Not uncommonly one of the adult children will state that he or she wants "...dad kept alive at all costs", against the wishes of the rest of the family. The physician has almost no choice to comply until all family members are in agreement. At this point it may take up to 5 days or more to get everyone in agreement.

♦ **Whose death is this, anyways!**

When death is all but inevitable, occurring within a few days to many months, it is now that the physician faces his greatest challenge.

**Intervening, even briefly, between our fellow creatures
And their suffering or death
Is the most authentic answer to the question of our humanity!
Howard Sackler**

This is our calling, our covenant. It doesn't stop when we can no longer cure or suppress a disease. We are still dealing with the whole person, a person whose physical condition is causing his death—a person who is suffering emotionally and physically.

**Treating a disease is win-lose
Treating a person is win-win!
Patch Adams**

Explaining the seriousness of the situation is never easy and some physicians do it in a very compassionate manner, like they would want it done to them or a member of their family, delivering the news with 'a heavy heart.' Unfortunately, some physicians delight in giving bad news; it gives them a sense of power, not unlike the neighborhood gossip who loves to tell about the bad things (never the good things) happening to a neighbor or a mutual 'friend'. Sit with the patient and the family. Lead the discussion by asking questions and then listen deeply. How is this affecting the whole patient? The family?

Breaking bad news is never easy but physicians must do this not infrequently. All of us develop ways of doing this, most commonly from our role models. When a physician withholds bad news, it diminishes the patient's autonomy. One way is the method devised by Baile and colleagues using the SPIKES mnemonic: Setting up, Perception, Invitation, Knowledge, Emotions, and Strategy/summary.

SPIKES

The **s**etting up stage begins by sitting down with the patient and the family in a private place, making eye contact, touching the patient appropriately. Watch your body language—'all eyes are on you!' Compassion is a must. If this is occurring in an academic center, no more than one other member of the house staff should be present.

The **p**erception of the patient involves knowing what the patient already knows. Ask them if they understand what their symptoms might be due to or why the biopsy or surgery or the imaging procedure was done. This allows you to adjust your explanation along these lines. (Ideally, before any diagnostic tests are done the patient should be told about the possibility of something 'not good' being found if that is in the differential diagnosis, even if it is a small chance. If that is the case, it is important to get the results back to the patient as soon as possible, including benign or non malignant finding. This is part of the Platinum Rule of Medicine.)

Invitation to break bad news by getting the patient's permission to share the findings of the current situation, i.e., "I'd like to share with you what we know. I wish I had better news for you." Saying, "I'm sorry, I have bad news…" is not as acceptable. Then proceed from there. Unnecessary bluntness isn't appropriate. <u>Never</u> take away hope. Don't express pity.

♦ **We can treat but we can't cure!**

Knowledge of the situation should be tailored to the patient's comprehension of the medical facts and given in small increments. Allow them to ask questions as you move along. Make sure they understand.

Emotions of the patient and the family must be recognized all through this; allowing periods of silence lets the bad news sink in. There is nothing wrong with just sitting silently for 2 to 5 minutes, maybe holding the patient's hand. Many people, on first hearing bad news, go 'numb', almost 'brain-dead'. You may have to repeat your answers several times before they understand. Empathy on the part of the physician is critical here.

If the family isn't present at this initial visit of bad news, be sure you eventually tell them what you told the patient. And record in the record what you told the patient and what your plans are. It is important that the health care team be kept in the loop because, if the patient is in the hospital, the nurses are going to be confronted with a lot of questions when you are gone. Ask the patient or a family member to write down the questions for you to answer later.

You need to explain measures to the health care team that may be a little out of the ordinary in a dying patient that is likely to die in the next few days or weeks, such as why you are starting an antibiotic or giving a unit of blood.

Strategy/summary sets the stage for revisiting the patient and answering many questions that occurred after receiving the news. Never say "…nothing more can be done." Comfort/care is doing something and explain this.

In an academic center the staff physician should go back after rounds and see the patient alone or with just the resident (or one medical student) in charge to answer more questions. This is part of the residents' and medical students' education. Ask the resident(s) what he or she told the patient and the family when he made his rounds. You should always be on the same page.

> From a physician writing in a major medical journal about the terminal illness of his father when the writer was only 12 years old: *A doctor called. He spoke very briefly and matter of factly, like a post master calling to say a package had arrived, and said my father had acute leukemia...I can't remember much about the doctors who cared for him over the next 4 months, not even their names. We hardly saw them.*

At this point or sometime in the near future, the physician must inquire into what the patient's wishes are, either in his Advanced Directive or verbally, record this in the medical record, and be sure the family all agrees.

Dying is not only a medical event, it is also a social experience. Our country now is as much a melting pot as it was 2 or 3 centuries ago, except now there is a much wider diversity of cultures represented and each has its own cultural mores. Too make matters worse, many don't speak English. Some cultures want everything heroic done—it's a sign of respect. Others don't like to be told the truth, making it very difficult to refer a patient with metastatic cancer to an oncologist. More often than not the patient knows what is happening, further eroding the trust in their physician. *If you don't know the cultural mores, ask one of the senior members of the family, their clergy, or look it up on a web site.*

Establish a decision maker in the family, in addition to the patient, to get directions on what is best to do.

Knowing their cultural mores is respect. Don't tell them what you would do unless you have established mutual trust and this isn't easy to do if you just met the patient today for the first time!

People aren't afraid of death; but they are afraid of dying!

**I'm not afraid of death. I just don't want
To be there when it happens!**
Woody Allen

We talk of a good death, of dying well. This means the same thing to everyone, no matter what the culture. It is synonymous with dignity, control, autonomy and especially pain and symptom control. Rummons et al write in the Mayo Clinic Proceedings of the Quality of Life of the terminally ill which includes the physical, psychological, social and spiritual aspects of health. They list 4 factors that are extremely important: depression, anxiety, shortness of breath and sense of well being. These must be dealt with as well as pain which is now considered the 5th vital sign. Over 50% of terminally ill patients have a significant depression. It may be higher.

♦ **A good death—being the same person dying as you were when alive!**

I would add a phrase that I have almost never seen in all my review of this subject and that is *peace of mind*. You can't have a sense of well being or a good death without this. This is the essence of spirituality.

Before a good death, with peace of mind, can occur, the patient needs to say 5 things:

1) Forgive me
2) I forgive you
3) Thank you
4) I love you
5) Goodbye

Any person, dying or otherwise, uses the mechanism of hope to obtain peace and happiness. Faith then becomes the unconditional substance of things hoped for, the evidence of things not seen.

Details of an estate should be taken care of and some feel better if they can still make a contribution to society. There is always concern how the death will affect the family that must be dealt with.

Many people, at least in this country, want to know how long they have to live. The public needs to know that the physician unintentionally significantly under or over estimates the time left. In spite of 'your need to know', be respectful of the fact that even very experienced physicians have difficulty with this. Most prefer not to offer a 'guesstimate', unless it is fairly broad. And caution the residents or other attendings taking care of this patient about this. Discrepant specific estimates from the health care team will really confuse the patient and the family.

The unexpected death of one of your patients such as in an emergency medical department or ICU or anywhere in the hospital is always difficult. You need to be prepared for this because, by definition, it happens quickly. You need to think this out before confronting the family. Your words should be well thought out. Know your own emotions. You can follow a variation of the SPIKES format with compassion being your message. "I have bad news—your husband died totally unexpectedly, we think it was due to ___. We did everything we could think of to save him. We had no warning this would happen." In this situation you have to get right to the bad news—it is totally unexpected.

Now you need to be silent for the next few minutes, unless of course, you are answering questions from the family. They need time for this to sink in. You will have to go through this as more family is notified and comes in. Record in the record exactly what happened to the patient and what you told the family. Some family may not arrive while you are still available, leaving the resident or nurses to answer their questions.

Be prepared that some family members might express anger. Handle this with calmness and compassion. Let them ventilate. Notify the referring or primary physician if you are not it. And if an autopsy is done be sure to call a member of the family right away to give the preliminary results.

Hope, what does it mean to the terminally ill? In preparing to give the annual Roger C. Bone MD Memorial Lecture at Rush Medical College it gave me an opportunity to review his many publications on end of life issues. Roger was a world class scientist; then in 1994 he was found to have cancer. This, of course, changed his whole outlook on life and he began writing about this experience as well as his philosophy about life in general. He brings with these writings end of life issues out in the open, both as a patient and as a well known physician, who soon realized that he had metastatic disease.

His several publications, monograph and 55 minute videotape (available through the American College of Chest Physicians, Northbrook, Illinois) beautifully and poignantly describe what it means to be dying, and this is by a physician whose special interest was intensive care medicine where he had seen many patients die in spite of the best efforts of a team of experts.

In his writings he emphasizes that you prioritize what is important to you—it should be your family and friends and your happiness. As I stated previously, by doing this you will be a better physician, work smarter, and probably accomplish more.

What I think I learned the most in preparing for Roger's lecture was what the word **hope** might mean to the terminally ill. At this point in time the mechanism of denial of disease has passed.

Cure if you can, alleviate and comfort always, and
Never take away hope!
Edward Trudeau

Almost every author who has written on death and dying, and end of life issues, mentions hope, or at least alludes to it. Hope arouses a passion for the possible.

♦ **Hope...is not the optimistic conviction that something will turn out well, but the certainty that something makes sense, regardless of how it turns out!** (Vaclav Havel)

Roger talked about his maintaining hope, and this was when he knew of his metastases to the brain, lungs and bones, and had failed his fourth different trial of chemotherapy.

I wished I had asked Roger when he knew he was dying what he thought hope meant to him. Did he think he might be one in a million who would go into spontaneous remission in spite of widespread metastases? Or that someone was working on a truly remarkable new drug that would cure him? As an experienced clinician he knew that if such a drug were on the horizon, it would take 1 to 5 years to clear the FDA hurdles just to get to human trials.

Hope means different things to the non terminally ill patient versus those terminally ill—the hope in someone who hopes his cholesterol is lower as a result of his diet is much different in someone dying. In the former situation, that person has a lot of control over the desired result whereas the terminally ill patient has little or no control and is just another reminder to him or her of the frustration and despair associated with the loss of autonomy. We take for granted the control and autonomy we have over our lives until we lose this control, leading to a very depersonalized and helpless feeling.

So, what did Roger mean when he talked of the importance of maintaining hope? For many years I have wondered about this and wasn't satisfied that everyone holding on to hope, especially those with metastatic disease, actually thought that they'd survive. Or were they only hoping for more weeks or months of life than they have been lead to believe they had?

Hope is not a way out,
It is a way through!

Robert Frost

Robert Frost's insight gave me my answer. I interpret this to mean that 'the way through' is the peaceful passage with dignity and peace of mind, and without pain and suffering to the next life, whatever your spiritual beliefs lead you to believe it is. Most people dying feel that they've lost their dignity, and as stated earlier, many people aren't afraid of death, just of dying. What I think they fear almost more than anything is fear of *abandonment*, especially by their physician(s), which must lead to an almost indescribable loneliness. A *way through* without being abandoned by your physician(s), family and friends.

> In an article published in a leading medical journal, a physician describes his father's death, his father also being a physician who took care of hundreds of patients who died. The author asked his father what his greatest fear was and he replied, *That I will be left alone in a corner to die*. His fear was that of abandonment.

Some patients assume that a promise (or implicit assumption) that by complying with all the physician's recommendations for tests, chemotherapy, quitting smoking, that they will benefit from treatment. This is a transference of the power of healing to the physician, further raising the specter of hope. The physician needs to be as honest as possible with the patient without offering false hopes.

There are nearly 3500 books on record with the reference to hope. Hope is both a noun and a verb. The Thesaurus does not list an alternative single word that has the same meaning or connotation. But the word hope that I am writing about does have an implication of dignity in its potential fulfillment. It is definitely a necessity in coping, and does generate some energy. It is also associated with pleasant feelings, a peace of mind that helps ease some of the burden. Hope, in addition to not wanting to be abandoned, is transcendent to spirituality.

After trying to put all this together is, I think, that hope in the terminally ill patient can mean several things:

HOPE	NO HOPE
A feeling that someone cares	Abandoned
Dignity	Loneliness
Control/autonomy	Hopeless, loss of control
An antidepressant	Depersonalized
Energy	Giving up
Coping mechanism	Negative attitude
Pleasant feeling/peace of mind	Depression
Strength of character	Suffering
Positive attitude	

Certainly, a chance to survive would be high priority but after denial is no longer a factor, hope can mean all those things in the left hand column.

♦ **The very presence of my physician meant so much to me, it gave me hope!**

From an article in the New York Times: *The whole time he was in the hospice center, he was never visited by his doctor. No matter that the occasional presence of a physician during those final weeks could have brought real comfort, even if no cure.*

Your patient needs you now more than ever. You need to tell him or her that you won't abandon them. Empathetic words like, "I cannot begin to know what you are going through, but you must know I care." "Is there anything you want to talk about?", convey a tremendous message of caring, and done while sitting at eye level with the patient, leaning forward, looking them in the eye, and holding their hand.

For many terminally ill patients, the thought of giving up hope makes them believe it will lead to death that much sooner, and by maintaining hope, may prolong life and give them some time. Maintaining hope, a final cling to dignity, tells his family and friends that he still has strength of character, whereas, giving up hope (if it hasn't been completely taken away from him by now) is perceived as 'giving up', a humiliating sign of weakness in the patient's mind.

I have been with many patients who openly talked about their imminent death without despair, with a positive attitude! As I look back none of these people had any sense of abandonment. They were in control.

I think another aspect to hope in the terminally ill patient is that as long as there is hope they can try to maintain this positive attitude. Roger mentions this by saying, "Hope is our last defense against despair." In this situation you likely either have hope or no hope; it's not likely that there is much in between. With no hope, nothing is left but negative thoughts, with further depression. Most of these patients are already depressed. Hope allows them to suppress or fight off what would be an almost unbearable despair. There is no effective antidepressant medication for this kind of despair when there is no hope. Poorly controlled pain further contributes to this despair.

The tragic sinking of the Russian nuclear submarine *Kursk* ironically occurred shortly after the publication of a book on the first successful undersea rescue of 31 men in 1939 from an American submarine, the *Squalus*, sunk in over 200 feet of water. In a Washington Post interview with the author Peter Maas he described the never before tested bell device put together by Swede Momsen and how, through Morse code messages tapped out on the hull of the sub, the surviving 31 men were told that Momsen was on his way with a device to help them. Survivors later described their hopes and that *the idea that someone cares, was a more powerful opiate to despair than the idea of the omnipotence of technology when the chips are down!* (exclamation mark is mine—that quote says a lot).

Roger Bone made an interesting statement that I didn't pick up the meaning of until I read it a second time. He was writing about his experience as a patient in an oncology unit where he and 12 to 15 other patients were receiving chemotherapy. He noted: *The nurses there are the closest thing to angels on this earth. Over the last several months, I have watched them shower their patients with genuine love and compassion. I have never seen anything but smiles, empathy, and optimistic attitudes from the nursing staff. They have behaved this way even when a patient has been quite difficult.*

What I think Roger is describing is that these nurses were delivering hope. Some might think the terms 'smiling' and 'optimism' are inappropriate in this setting, but they're not. The nurses were using their body language to express to the patients something that maybe no one else had offered them—hope! They weren't promising anything to their patients—they didn't have to. They knew that false hopes erode trust and impair further effective communication. As I have stated before, the art of medicine can be learned, but it can't be taught. These nurses were allowing the patients and their families to learn about hope; they weren't teaching it!

> **Physicians, family, friends, the clergy and**
> **Members of the health care team**
> **Can offer hope**
> **But only the physician can take it away!**

Cure if you can...but never take away hope. We have to ask ourselves now, how do we want our physician to deliver hope to us, to our family?

Why can't all physicians deliver hope, to all their patients, and not just to those dying? Certainly, never take it away!

Spirituality means different things to different people. *Faith is one of the 6 Fs in my Balance in Life.* It can include religiosity which is a person's adherence to the beliefs and practices of organized religion. Only in the last century did the science of medicine and religion separate. Religion of the patient was never discussed at any time in the era of my training. Now in many medical schools the curriculum contains courses in religion and spirituality as well as complementary and alternative medicine. Surveys show that patients want their doctor to ask about their religious or spiritual views and that the majority of adults believe that religion and spirituality are important in health matters.

> ♦ **There are no atheists in a fox hole!** (Ernie Pyle, WW II correspondent)

I'm discussing spirituality in this section on end-of-life issues because for many people this is when it becomes a major strength and comfort in their lives. But many people find spirituality in times of stress or when 'mastering' the Art of Living and simplifying their lives.

> **God's finger touched him, and he slept!**
> **Alfred Tennyson**

Spirituality is a person's search for meaning in life, a purpose of belonging to something larger than oneself that is worthwhile, and may or may not include a connectedness to a higher power or a supreme Being (religion).

Spirituality can be a source of inner strength, bringing a peace of an awareness of reserves from beyond ourselves, so that our strength is not so much in us as it is through us. The Dalai Lama describes it as a sense of commonality among all living things.

> ♦ **The highest thoughts are those least dependent on language!**

165

Civility is a form of spirituality, the practice of accepting all others with mutual respect and treating them accordingly, especially with acts of kindness.

Some describe spirituality as the striving for, or the ability to, transcend the boundaries of the familiar. It is felt to be more of an individualistic rather than a conformist approach to life's experiences. The higher power might be found in the beauty of nature, in a peace of mind, or music, or the bonding of family and friends. Faith is a belief in the substance of things hoped for.

Studies using the SPECT (single photon emission computerized tomography) and PET scans of the brain disclose an enhancement of areas of the left frontal cortex during deep meditation or prayer while at the same time another area of the cortex responsible for the person's spatial orientation, his contact with the outside world, shuts down. It requires active thinking and practice to reach the level of concentrations necessary for this.

The people having this kind of experience all say about the same thing:

- *A oneness with all of nature or with all of the universe*
- *A sense that "I", the person, was not alone or isolated but a part of everything around me, a connectedness*
- *Timelessness*
- *That everything is one and infinite*
- *A wholeness, unlike anything I've ever felt before*
- *Harmony with the universe, with nature*
- *Feeling of knowing beyond knowledge*
- *In unity with everything, a communion with all*
- *A feeling of peace*

Many people achieve spirituality through solitude, best exemplified in the writings of Thoreau through his experiences of living alone in the woods. To appreciate solitude in its completeness, you must be willing to abandon the concept of yourself as the center of the universe and become one with the universe itself. As a result we become a part of something larger, acquiring a peacefulness that is not a loneliness.

You can see how some people have an affinity with nature as Nature, even to those without a spirituality with nature. Everywhere is beautiful, even the deserts, barren mountains, Antarctica landscape. They see the work of a supreme Being in commune with Nature. Any object in Nature takes on a life of its own, animate or not, and is appreciated as such. This could be dew reflected off a cobweb, the radiance of heat above the desert floor, the majesty of a mountain at sunset, the awesomeness of a violent storm.

Stephen Covey in *First Things First* Points out that nature is always changing, most notable in the storms and the seasons, but it always follows the law. It teaches balance through irregular consistencies, and controlled chaos. It reminds us that there are laws and that through these, it (nature) is ultimately in control, giving us a sense of comfort that *there is order in the universe.*

> **See how Nature—trees, grass—grows in silence; see the**
> **Stars, the moon, the sun, how they move in silence....**
> **We need silence to be able to touch souls!**
> **Mother Theresa**

I would add to that that we also need silence to grow.

◆ **Silence is a powerful weapon!** (Sir William Osler)

The neuropathways that light up with these intense experiences beg the question, "How did they get there?" Most (all?) neuropathways are inherent, or a result of life experiences. Do we unknowingly create this ethereal world in our brain, or did God? The answer can be what you want it to be. No matter what, it is totally harmless, always positive, and I think, potentially responsible for what must be an almost indescribable peace of mind when you allow it to happen.

Ernie Pyle's 'no atheists in a fox hole' phenomenon certainly acts as a coping mechanism when probably nothing else would. Many a soldier has described the sensation of someone else being with them when alone in battlefield situations.

I wonder if in the last stages of life, this intense spiritual experience as seen on SPECT scans becomes a part of the dying process and transfers the 'hope of no abandonment' to a spiritual being (?Being) to carry the person through to the next stage in peace and with dignity. I happen to believe in a life after death, but I do not believe a physician should impose his or her beliefs on to the patient. It is imperative, however, that the physician support the patient's belief.

Maintaining communication with the patient and the family as well as the health care team is imperative, and doing so in a language that the patient can understand. Compassionate behavior is more appreciated by patients and families at end of life than good communication, but poor communication is the single most common complaint by the families when compassionate care is not delivered. One value of a hospice is that they do both.

The phrase 'above all do no harm' can be a misnomer if it means the physician does nothing. Comfort care, palliative care with dignity, is a minimum, focusing on improving the quality of life.

◆ **Sometimes the most we can offer the sufferer is to listen and comfort!**

By establishing trust through communication and your very presence, the patient will open up to you about his or her concerns. Suffering is more than pain and if you don't make a diagnosis of suffering, you can't treat it. Suffering includes a fear of the future. Ask about suffering; use your intuition. Observe the body language. Remember, it is an affliction of the person, not the body.

Are there symptoms worse than the pain? Are they sleeping OK? What are their worries about the family? Sit quietly with them. Touch. Listen—are they saying what they mean? Don't abandon them. Discuss practical things and spiritual beliefs. When they mention negative things, don't inappropriately reassure them that everything will be OK; instead, ask them a question.

♦ **You, the physician, are allowed to feel helpless at times!**

As the patient slips into an unresponsive state, the last 2 senses to diminish are hearing and touch. Familiar voices and touch probably help the patient further transcend to the spiritual dimension. Peaceful death bonds the family, their friends and the health care team together, through shared suffering, hope and spirituality.

At the time of death, we need to think more about the value of life. It's time to focus on the life of the deceased, not the last few days or weeks of his or her life, unless the family has some unanswered questions.

The physician's obligations don't stop here. He needs to deal with his own grief and the family's grief and frequently the grief of some of the health care team. If possible attend visitation or the funeral or memorial service. And always send a sympathy card or letter with a personal note.

Even if you haven't seen the patient in a while, it is still appropriate to express your sympathy, either in person or writing. Not doing this sends a negative message to the family and reflects negatively on the medical profession. If a team of housestaff cared for a patient, then all involved should sign the note or card.

It is important to remember the 5 stages of grief:

1) Denial. "No, not me!"
2) Anger. "Why me? What did I do to deserve this punishment!"
3) Bargaining. "I'll quit smoking!"
4) Depression. "I deserved this!" Stops communicating.
5) Acceptance. "I need to get my affairs in order and begin to say goodbye!"

Every grieving person must pass through all 5 stages. The length of each stage varies from person to person, but a prolonged stage of any of the first 4 might be considered as pathologic grief. Depression can last through the final acceptance stage, or it may disappear and return when hope is lost or pain remains uncontrolled.

The physician must ask himself or herself,

**"Did I take care of this patient's dying days
Like I would want myself or my family cared for?"**

CONCLUSION

I didn't initially plan a summary but I've learned so much from my reading of numerous books and articles as well as gelling my thoughts on rereading and rewriting this book, that I feel it is important to briefly summarize what I think are the important features that I would like you to remember. As you recall, the initial premise was to tell young physicians that they aren't as effective a physician if they aren't happy, aren't enjoying life, the Art of Living. As Brown said, *I finally figured out that the reason to be alive is to enjoy it.*

Balance in your life is absolutely critical, beginning now. You have no promise for tomorrow, no one does. Don't postpone joy. Your life is your career, your work is part of your life. Your priorities must be family, friends, fun, ...and work.

The respect for you—yourself—as well as your health takes parallel high priority to family, friends and fun. You can't take your wellness for granted. Depression, if it occurs, comes insidiously and affects everything you do and everyone around you. It almost always can be effectively treated. Maintain a heightened awareness for this in yourself as well as those around you. Deal with it.

We are creatures of habit. We rely on 'assumptive thinking' without actually and truly reflecting on the data before us, or the potential consequences of what we are about to do. We live on automatic pilot. This can result in stupid actions. It takes work to become mindful of everything you are doing now, but with time mindfulness will become more automatic. This applies also to negative thinking—stop it! You have total control over this. A positive attitude will get you almost every where you want to be.

It wasn't until I was over half way through writing this book that I realized that I hadn't once mentioned the word happiness. It turned out to be one of my longest sections. Happiness should be the sine quo non of enjoying life, but it must come from within—you alone are responsible for this. But you must work at it. An attitudinal intent to be happy is imperative. It should be a fairly constant mind-think. It can't be done without smiling, without a sense of gratitude and appreciation. The value of a smile is incalculable. The best way to be happy is to make others happy. *You can't expect your children and grandchildren to be happy if you aren't.*

A sense of humor is absolutely essential as is adopting a positive attitude.

Delvina Dahlhumer (from Minnesota, no less) was interviewed on her 113th birthday shortly before she died of natural causes and was asked what she attributed her long life to. She said, "Nothing ever bothered me." For those of us who are bothered by everything, it'll just seem like we are 113!

I've become even more impressed with the importance of calling people by their name; you connect with them and they feel good about this.

Lowering your expectations of people won't lead to disappointment. Authors writing on happiness, wisdom, equanimity, maturity, mindfulness, and emotional intelligence all allude to this. This allows you to be less reliant on others for your happiness.

I've listed so many 'imperatives' in what I think are important in the Art of Living, but effective communication is critical, especially the art of listening. Be aware that your body language can reveal your attitude, your level of unhappiness, your anger (outright or suppressed), your self-esteem.

Finally, if I have to pick what I think is the most important thing I've learned, I would select the value of the practice of **kindness**, not only to the people you work with and your patients, I mean everyone around you that you interact with or just coincidentally encounter in the street or the other end of the phone. And also to yourself. Make being kind a philosophy of your life. One act of kindness leaves the world a little bit better. Remember, *it's fun to be kind!*

All human beings experience guilt, frustration, fear, shame. We need to accept this in ourselves and others and help each other. *We are all in this together.* An act of kindness is infectious; the more you do the better you feel, and the kinder you get. It builds. It contributes to equanimity and a good self-esteem. Be a little kinder than necessary. The Dalai Lama says that his religion is kindness.

In order to develop more kindness begin each day with a *positive attitude*. Then add a *smile. Kindness* and *respect* will follow automatically, as will *equanimity* and *happiness*, leading to an even more positive attitude. I describe this as the *Circle of Happiness.*

Be the best you can be, but without striving for perfection. Be a role model to everyone and a mentor to at least someone besides your children. And don't be afraid to be yourself.

I close with Ralph Waldo Emerson's poem that so beautifully portrays what I have been trying to say in this book:

To laugh often and much;
To win the respect
Of intelligent people
And the affection
Of children;
To earn the appreciation
Of honest critics
And endure the betrayal of false friends.
To appreciate beauty;
To find the best in others;
To leave the world
A bit better
Whether by a healthy child,
A garden patch or
A redeemed social condition;
To know that even one life has breathed easier
Because you have lived.
This is to have succeeded.
****

Printed in the United States
by Baker & Taylor Publisher Services